日本語 NOW
NihonGO NOW!

NihonGO NOW! is a beginning-level courseware package that takes a performed-culture approach to learning Japanese. This innovative approach balances the need for an intellectual understanding of structural elements with multiple opportunities to experience the language within its cultural context.

From the outset, learners are presented with samples of authentic language that are context-sensitive and culturally coherent. Instructional time is used primarily to rehearse interactions that learners of Japanese are likely to encounter in the future, whether they involve speaking, listening, writing, or reading.

Level 1 comprises two textbooks with accompanying activity books. These four books in combination with audio files allow instructors to adapt a beginning-level course, such as the first year of college Japanese, to their students' needs. They focus on language and modeled behavior, providing opportunities for learners to acquire language through performance templates. Online resources provide additional support for both students and instructors. Audio files, videos, supplementary exercises, and a teachers' manual are available at www.routledge.com/9781138304147.

NihonGO NOW! Level 1 Volume 1 Activity Book provides a wealth of communicative exercises and assessment tools for students working through the first semester of the *NihonGO NOW!* course.

Mari Noda is Professor of Japanese at The Ohio State University.

Patricia J. Wetzel is Emerita Professor of Japanese at Portland State University.

Ginger Marcus is Professor of the Practice of Japanese Language at Washington University in St. Louis.

Stephen D. Luft is Lecturer of Japanese at the University of Pittsburgh.

Shinsuke Tsuchiya is Assistant Professor of Japanese at Brigham Young University.

Masayuki Itomitsu is Associate Professor of Japanese at Linfield College.

日本語 NOW!
NihonGO NOW!

Performing Japanese Culture
Level 1 Volume 1
Activity Book

Mari Noda, Patricia J. Wetzel, Ginger Marcus,
Stephen D. Luft, Shinsuke Tsuchiya,
and Masayuki Itomitsu

Routledge
Taylor & Francis Group

LONDON AND NEW YORK

First published 2021
by Routledge
2 Park Square, Milton Park, Abingdon, Oxon OX14 4RN

and by Routledge
52 Vanderbilt Avenue, New York, NY 10017

Routledge is an imprint of the Taylor & Francis Group, an informa business

© 2021 Mari Noda, Patricia J. Wetzel, Ginger Marcus, Stephen D. Luft, Shinsuke Tsuchiya, and Masayuki Itomitsu

The right of Mari Noda, Patricia J. Wetzel, Ginger Marcus, Stephen D. Luft, Shinsuke Tsuchiya, and Masayuki Itomitsu to be identified as authors of this work has been asserted by them in accordance with sections 77 and 78 of the Copyright, Designs and Patents Act 1988.

British Library Cataloguing-in-Publication Data
A catalogue record for this book is available from the British Library

Library of Congress Cataloging-in-Publication Data
Names: Noda, Mari, author.
Title: Nihongo now! : performing Japanese culture / Mari Noda, Patricia J. Wetzel, Ginger Marcus, Stephen D. Luft, Shinsuke Tsuchiya, Masayuki Itomitsu.
Description: New York : Routledge, 2020. | Includes bibliographical references. | Contents: Level 1, volume 1. Textbook—Level 1, volume 1. Activity book—Level 1, volume 2. Textbook—Level 1, volume 2. Activity book. | In English and Japanese.
Identifiers: LCCN 2020026010 (print) | LCCN 2020026011 (ebook) | ISBN 9780367509279 (level 1, volume 1 ; set ; hardback) | ISBN 9780367508494 (level 1, volume 1 ; set ; paperback) | ISBN 9781138304123 (level 1, volume 1 ; textbook ; hardback) | ISBN 9781138304147 (level 1, volume 1 ; textbook ; paperback) | ISBN 9781138304277 (level 1, volume 1 ; activity book ; hardback) | ISBN 9781138304314 (level 1, volume 1 ; activity book ; paperback) | ISBN 780367509309 (level 1, volume 2 ; set ; hardback) | ISBN 9780367508531 (level 1, volume 2 ; set ; paperback) | ISBN 9780367483241 (level 1, volume 2 ; textbook ; hardback) | ISBN 9780367483210 (level 1, volume 2 ; textbook ; paperback) | ISBN 9780367483494 (level 1, volume 2 ; activity book ; hardback) | ISBN 9780367483364 (level 1, volume 2 ; activity book ; paperback) | ISBN 9780203730249 (level 1, volume 1 ; ebook) | ISBN 9780203730362 (level 1, volume 1 ; ebook) | ISBN 9781003051855 (level 1, volume 1 ; ebook) | ISBN 9781003039334 (level 1, volume 2 ; ebook) | ISBN 9781003039471 (level 1, volume 2 ; ebook) | ISBN 9781003051879 (level 1, volume 2 ; ebook)
Subjects: LCSH: Japanese language—Textbooks for foreign speakers—English. | Japanese language—Study and teaching—English speakers.
Classification: LCC PL539.5.E5 N554 2020 (print) | LCC PL539.5.E5 (ebook) | DDC 495.682/421—dc23
LC record available at https://lccn.loc.gov/2020026010
LC ebook record available at https://lccn.loc.gov/2020026011

ISBN: 978-1-138-30427-7 (hbk)
ISBN: 978-1-138-30431-4 (pbk)
ISBN: 978-0-203-73024-9 (ebk)

Typeset in Times New Roman
by Apex CoVantage, LLC

Visit the eResources: www.routledge.com/9781138304147

Contents

序幕 *Jomaku* Introduction

理解練習 *Rikai renshuu* Comprehension practice

0-1C What should you do?

Listen to the instructional expressions and select from the illustrations the one that represents the most appropriate response to each of the instructions.

Ex. 1. __d__	Ex. 2. __a__	3. __a.__	4. __b__	5. __d__
6. __c__	7. __e__	8. __f__	9. __g__	10. __j__
11. __h__	12. __g__	13. __i__	14. ____	15. ____
16. ____	17. __g__	18. __c__	19. __b__	20. ____

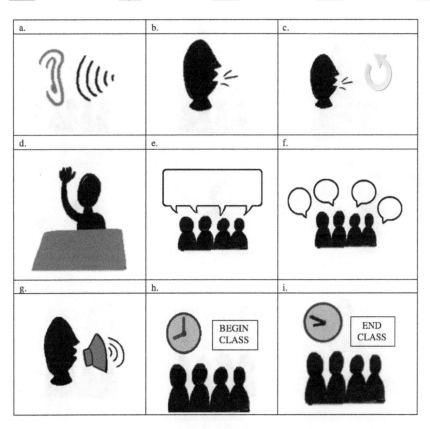

0-2C What should you do?

Listen to the instructional expressions and select from the illustrations the one that represents the most appropriate response to each of the instructions.

Ex. 1. __i__   Ex. 2. __k__   3. _____   4. _____   5. _____

6. _____   7. _____   8. _____   9. _____   10. _____

11. _____   12. _____   13. _____   14. _____   15. _____

16. _____   17. _____   18. _____   19. _____   20. _____

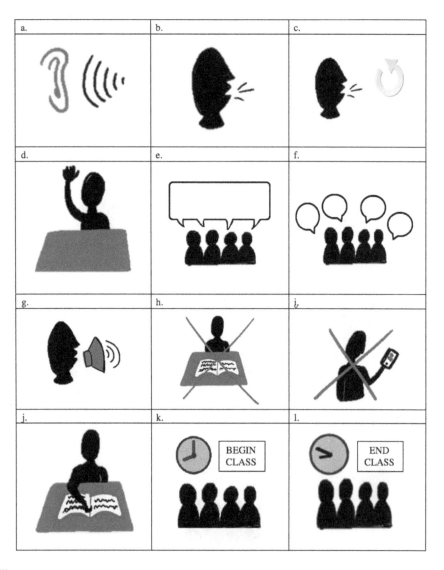

0-3C Mora count

Listen to groups of 4 words. All items in the same group have the same number of Japanese syllables, or morae, except one. Check the one item in each group that has a different number of morae from the others in the same group.

Ex. Group 1.	a. ✓	b. _____	c. _____	d. _____
Ex. Group 2.	a. _____	b. _____	c. ✗	d. ✓
Group 3.	a. _____	b. ✓	c. _____	d. ✓
Group 4.	a. ✓	b. _____	c. _____	d. _____
Group 5.	a. _____	b. _____	c. _____	d. ✓

0-4C Mora count (Same procedures as Practice 0-3C)

Ex. Group 1.	a. ✓	b. _____	c. _____	d. _____
Ex. Group 2.	a. _____	b. ✓	c. _____	d. _____
Group 3.	a. _____	b. _____	c. _____	d. _____
Group 4.	a. _____	b. _____	c. _____	d. _____
Group 5.	a. _____	b. _____	c. _____	d. _____

0-5C Mora count

Listen and identify the number of morae in each item.

Ex. 1. 2	Ex. 2. 3	3. 5	4. 4	5. 3
6. 6	7. 7	8. 4	9. 5	10. 4
11. 3	12. 6	13. 12	14. 4	15. _____

0-6C Mora count

Listen and identify the number of morae in each item.

Ex. 1. 4	Ex. 2. 4	3. _____	4. _____	5. _____
6. _____	7. _____	8. _____	9. _____	10. _____
11. _____	12. _____	13. _____	14. _____	15. _____

0-7C Accent

Listen to groups of 4 words. All items in the same group have the same accent patterns, except one. Check the one item in each group that has a different accent pattern from the others in the same group.

Ex. Group 1.	a. _____	b. _____	c. _____	d. __✓__
Ex. Group 2.	a. _____	b. _____	c. __✓__	d. _____
Group 3.	a. __✓__	b. _____	c. _____	d. _____
Group 4.	a. _____	b. _____	c. _____	d. __✓__
Group 5.	a. _____	b. __✓__	c. _____	d. _____

0-8C Accent

Listen to the short sequences and identify the pitch patterns, using H for high and L for low pitch.

Ex. 1. _HLL_ Ex. 2. _HLL_ 3. _HHH_ 4. _HLL_ 5. _LLL_

6. _LH_ 7. _HL_ 8. _HLH_ 9. _LH_ 10. _LL_

0-9C Accent

Listen to the short sequences and identify the pitch patterns, using H for high and L for low pitch.

Ex. 1. LHHHL Ex. 2. HLLLHHH 3. _LHHHL_ 4. _HLLH_ 5. _HLLL_

6. _HLLH_ 7. _HLLH_ 8. _HLHLH_ 9. _LHLLH_ 10. _LLHLL_

0-10C Intonation

Listen to groups of 4 items. All items in the same group have the same intonation patterns, except one. Check the one item in the group that has a different accent pattern from the others in the same group.

Ex. Group 1.	a. __✓__	b. _____	c. _____	d. _____
Ex. Group 2.	a. _____	b. __✓__	c. _____	d. _____
Group 3.	a. _____	b. _____	c. _____	d. _____
Group 4.	a. _____	b. _____	c. _____	d. __✓__
Group 5.	a. _____	b. _____	c. __✓__	d. _____

xx

実演練習 *Jitsuen renshuu* Performance Practice
<ruby>実演練習<rt>じつえんれんしゅう</rt></ruby>

 0-11P What would you say?

For each of the following, say a greeting based on the context. Then listen to the sample, and how the other person(s) respond(s).

Ex. 1.		You are seeing a teacher for the first time today. It is 9:30 a.m.	
You	おはようございます。	*Ohayoo gozaimasu.*	Good morning.
Teacher	おはようございます。	*Ohayoo gozaimasu.*	Good morning.
Ex. 2.		You are seeing your boss for the first time today. It is 9:00 a.m.	
You	おはようございます。	*Ohayoo gozaimasu.*	Good morning.
Boss	おはよう。	*Ohayoo.*	Good morning.

3. You are greeting everyone in the office when you arrive at work. It is 8:50 a.m.
4. You are visiting a community meeting for the first time. It's 3:00 p.m.
5. Your Japanese class has just finished, and you are passing by your instructor on your way out. It is 3:50 p.m.
6. You are visiting a student organization on campus for the first time. It's 10:00 a.m.
7. You are meeting up with your teacher to go to a reception together. It's 7:00 p.m.
8. You are about to give a presentation to a group of members of the community. It's 4:00 p.m.

Introduction 腕試し *Udedameshi* Tryout
<ruby>腕試し<rt>うでだめ</rt></ruby>

Greet a Japanese person, and bow as you greet the person.

よろしくお願いします。

Yoroshiku onegai shimasu.

Nice to meet you.

◆ Scene 1-1 練習 *Renshuu* Practice

理解練習 *Rikai renshuu* Comprehension practice

 ### 1-1-1C Identifying the actors (BTS 2)

Identify the two speakers in each exchange. If the speaker says a full name, write the full name using the same order for surname and first name as the speaker. The first speaker is male; the second speaker is female.

	First (male) speaker	Second (female) speaker
Ex. 1.	Kanda	Amy Wang
Ex. 2.	Sakamoto	Morris
3.		
4.		
5.		
6.		

実演練習 *Jitsuen renshuu* Performance practice

 ### 1-1-2P Checking if everybody is here (BTS 1, 2)

You are an intern at a company and have been asked to take attendance at a meeting. Say each name on the attendance sheet below aloud and then listen for a response. Use ○ to indicate that the person is present, and X to indicate absent. Pause the audio if necessary to give yourself time to say each name correctly.

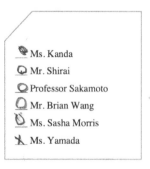

Ms. Kanda
Mr. Shirai
Professor Sakamoto
Mr. Brian Wang
Ms. Sasha Morris
Ms. Yamada

2

Ex. 1.

You	神田さん。	*Kanda-san.*	Kanda-san.
Ms. Kanda	はい。	*Hai.*	Here!

Ex. 2.

You	白井さん。	*Shirai-san.*	Shirai-san.
Mr. Shirai	はい。	*Hai.*	Here!

1-1 腕試し *Udedameshi* Tryout

Call your Japanese teacher by name to get his/her attention, then greet your teacher.

よろしくお願いします。

◆ Scene 1-2 練習 *Renshuu* Practice

理解練習 *Rikai renshuu* Comprehension practice

1-2-1C What's going on? (BTS 1, 3)

How is *hai* はい used in each of the following conversations? Select from:

a. Affirmative response ('that's right')
b. Handing something over ('here you go')
c. Accepting something handed to you ('got it')
d. Showing you are in attendance ('here' or 'present')

In this exercise, you may hear unfamiliar words, just as you would when speaking Japanese outside of the classroom since others won't know what you've studied. This is a chance for you to practice using what you do know to get an idea of what's going on.

Ex. 1.   This conversation occurs at a welcome party.   _____b_____
Ex. 2.   This conversation occurs in a classroom.   _____c_____
   3.   This conversation occurs at a welcome party.   _____a_____
   4.   This conversation occurs in a classroom.   _____d_____
   5.   This conversation occurs in an office.   _____b_____

実演練習 *Jitsuen renshuu* Performance practice

1-2-2P What would you say?

Imagine what you would say in each situation and say it aloud. Then, listen to the audio and put a check next to the option that best matches what you came up with.

Ex. 1.   Your pen ran out of ink, but your friend Amy came to the rescue with one of her pens. You want to thank her as you return her pen to her.   a._____ b._____ c._____ d. _✓_

Ex. 2.   You invited your friend over, and your friend has just arrived at your door.   a._____ b._✓_ c._____ d._____

   3.   You asked your professor to write a recommendation letter for you and she kindly agreed.   a._____ b._____ c._____

4. You are meeting with a professor who wrote a reference letter for you. You just reported to your professor that you received the scholarship you applied for with her support.
a._____ b._____ c._____

5. At a reception, you picked up a glass and the server handed you a paper napkin.
a._____ b._____ c._____

◆ Scene 1-3 練習 *Renshuu* Practice

実演練習 *Jitsuen renshuu* Performance practice

1-3-1P *Onegai-shimasu* (BTS 6)

For each of the following situations, if it would be appropriate to say *onegai-shimasu* お願いします write "Y." If not, write "N."

__Y__	Ex. 1.	You are in a shop and would like to talk to the salesclerk, but don't see the salesclerk around.
__N__	Ex. 2.	You have accidentally bumped into someone as you are walking through the train station.
Y	3.	You asked a friend if you could borrow a pencil, and your friend has just given you the pencil.
N	4.	An intern at work has offered to make some copies for you, and you would like him to do it.
N	5.	It is 9:30 a.m. and you are seeing a friend for the first time today.
Y	6.	You would like a professor to sign a document for you.
N	7.	A cashier at a supermarket has asked if you would like a bag, and you would like one.

◆ Scene 1-4 練習 *Renshuu* Practice

実演練習 *Jitsuen renshuu* Performance practice

 1-4-1P What would you say?

Imagine what you would say in each situation and say it aloud. Then, listen to the audio and put a check next to the option that best matches what you came up with.

Ex. 1. At a business meeting someone just presented her business card to you.   a._____ b._✓_ c._____

Ex. 2. Your teacher is taking attendance and has just called your name.   a._✓_ b._____ c._____

3. You are helping out at a reception desk at an event. You are handing a name badge to the attendee who just checked in.   a._____ b._✓_ c._____

4. Someone is waving in your direction and calling your name.   a._____ b._____ c._✓_

5. You have just given your business card to a new acquaintance.   a._____ b._✓_ c._✓_

7

◆ Scene 1-5 練習 *Renshuu* Practice

理解練習 *Rikai renshuu* Comprehension practice

1-5-1C What are they saying?

Write the letter of the word that you hear. If the word can be used to thank someone, write "Y" in the parentheses; otherwise, write "N."

Ex.			Ex.						
1.	c	(Y)	2.	b	(N)	3.	___ ( )	4.	___ ( )
5.	___	( )	6.	___	( )	7.	___ ( )	8.	___ ( )

a. *Doozo* / どうぞ
b. *Yoroshiku* / よろしく
c. *Arigatoo* / ありがとう
d. *Arigatoo gozaimasu* / ありがとうございます
e. *Sayoonara* / さようなら
f. *Arigatoo gozaimashita* / ありがとうございました
g. *Ohayoo* / おはよう

実演練習 *Jitsuen renshuu* Performance practice

1-5-2P What would you say?

Imagine what you would say in each situation and say it aloud. Then listen to how the other person reacts.

Ex. 1.	On your way to class in the morning, you have run into a friend in the hallway at school.		
You	おはよう。	*Ohayoo.*	Good morning.
Friend	おはよう。	*Ohayoo.*	Good morning.
Ex. 2.	It's 6:00 p.m. and your supervisor says that you may go home.		
You	では、失礼します。	*De wa shitsuree-shimasu.*	I'll be go ahead and excuse myself.
Supervisor	はい。	*Hai.*	Okay.

3. You have just met someone who will be helping you with your Japanese for the first time.
4. You've just called your new colleague by the wrong name.
5. A student younger than you gave you a snack.
6. You have run into one of your supervisors in the hallway in the morning.
7. Your instructor just announced that class is over.

理解練習 *Rikai renshuu* Comprehension practice

 1-6-1C What's going on?

In each conversation, listen to Brian and select the description that tells what he is doing. Use each description only once.

Ex. 1. __c__   Ex. 2. __a__

    3. _____   4. _____   5. _____   6. _____

a. Bidding farewell.
b. Responding to a request.
c. Thanking someone for a meal.
d. Entering an office.
e. Offering something.
f. Receiving something with gratitude.

実演練習 *Jitsuen renshuu* Performance practice

 1-6-2P Responding appropriately

Read the context, listen to the speaker, and then provide a response.

Ex. 1.		Your supervisor invites you to enter his office.	
Supervisor	どうぞ。	*Doozo.*	Come in.
You	失礼します。	*Shitsuree-shimasu.*	Thank you.
Ex. 2.		You and your host mother just finished eating.	
Host mother	ごちそうさま。	*Gochisoosama.*	Thank you.
You	ごちそうさまでした。	*Gochisoosama deshita.*	Thank you.

    3. Your senior co-worker (*senpai*) greets you in the morning.
    4. Your homestay mother invites you to begin eating.

◆ Scene 1-7 練習 *Renshuu* Practice
れんしゅう

理解練習 *Rikai renshuu* Comprehension practice
り かいれんしゅう

1-7-1C Listening for the name

Listen to the self-introductions and try to catch the name of the person. Write each person's name.

	Person's name
Ex. 1.	Sasha Morris
Ex. 2.	Suzuki Akira
3.	Hiroshi Ai
4.	Kenta Kanu
5.	Karou Sakamoto
6.	Ma Jondes
7.	Shiori Measo

1-7-2C Finding the one that doesn't belong

Listen to each group of items, a, b, c, and d. All items in each group except one share something in common in terms of their meaning or function in a conversation. Identify the one that doesn't fit by placing a circle (○) next to it.

Ex. Group 1.	a._____	b._____	c._____	d.__○__
Ex. Group 2.	a.__○__	b._____	c._____	d._____
Group 3.	a._____	b._____	c._____	d._____
Group 4.	a._____	b._____	c._____	d._____
Group 5.	a._____	b._____	c._____	d._____

11

◆ Scene 1-8 練習 *Renshuu* Practice

理解実演練習 *Rikai jitsuen renshuu* Comprehension and performance practice

 1-8-1CP Mora count

Listen, repeat, and identify the number of morae (beats) in each item. You will hear each item twice.

Ex. 1. __5__   Ex. 2. __4__
  3. _____   4. _____   5. _____   6. _____   7. _____
  8. _____   9. _____   10. _____   11. _____   12. _____

実演練習 *Jitsuen renshuu* Performance practice

 1-8-2P What would you say?

Imagine what you would say in each situation and say it aloud. Then listen to how the other person reacts.

Ex. 1.	You just finished a lunch-box meal with your friend.		
You	ごちそうさま。	*Gochisoosama.*	Thank you.
Friend	ごちそうさま。	*Gochisoosama.*	Thank you.
Ex. 2.	A shopkeeper just handed you the item you purchased.		
You	どうも。	*Doomo.*	Thanks.
Shopkeeper	どうもありがとうございます。	*Doomo arigatoo gozaimasu.*	Thank you.

3. You are leaving home to go to school and your host mother is seeing you off.
4. Your homestay father is about to leave for work.
5. You are visiting a client who has just offered you a seat.
6. You are concluding your first meeting with your project team and want to indicate the end of the meeting.
7. Your teacher has told you that you can keep the document you were looking at.
8. You see someone who looks like Ichiro, your friend who is several years younger. You want to see if it really is Ichiro.

◆ Scene 1-9 練習 (れんしゅう) *Renshuu* Practice

理解実演練習 (りかいじつえんれんしゅう) *Rikai jitsuen renshuu*
Comprehension and performance practice

 1-9-1CP Mora count

Listen, repeat, and identify the number of morae (beats) in each item.

Ex. 1. __5__   Ex. 2. __4__   3. _____   4. _____   5. _____
  6. _____   7. _____   8. _____   9. _____   10. _____

実演練習 (じつえんれんしゅう) *Jitsuen renshuu* Performance practice

 1-9-2P Does that sound right?

For each situation, imagine how you would respond and say it aloud. Then, listen to the audio and indicate which of the four utterances best matches what you have imagined as appropriate.

Ex. 1. At roll call, your name has just been called.   a._____ b._○_ c._____ d._____
Ex. 2. You and your host family are about to begin dinner.   a._○_ b._____ c._____ d._____
3. You have just finished lunch with a friend.   a._____ b._____ c._____ d._____
4. You are leaving your office for a meeting out of town.   a._____ b._____ c._____ d._____
5. Class just ended and your classmate is leaving.   a._____ b._____ c._____ d._____

 1-9-3P What would you say?

Imagine what you would say in each situation and say it aloud. Then listen to how the other person reacts.

Ex. 1.   You are hosting a reception, and one of your clients is leaving.
You   ありがとうございました。   *Arigatoo gozaimashita.*   Thank you (for what you've done).

13

Client	どうもありがとうございま した。失礼します。	*Doomo arigatoo* *gozaimashita.* *Shitsuree-shimasu.*	Thank you. Excuse me.
Ex. 2.	A friend of yours is treating you to a meal, and you are about to start eating.		
You	いただきます。	*Itadakimasu.*	Thank you.
Friend	どうぞ。	*Doozo.*	Go ahead.

3. You and your friend are going to different classes now, but will be meeting up again later for lunch.
4. You are about to leave the office to go on a business trip.
5. You are taking a client out to eat, and the meal has just been brought out.
6. You are waving good-bye to a baby.

1-9 腕試し *Udedameshi* Tryout

Say goodbye to someone before you leave, using the appropriate leave-taking expression.

1-9

よろしくお願いします。

理解練習 *Rikai renshuu* Comprehension practice

 1-10-1C What's going on?

Listen to each phrase and indicate whether it would be said (a) as a greeting, (b) when you or someone else leaves, or (c) at meal time.

Ex. 1. ___a___   Ex. 2. ___b___
  3. _____   4. _____   5. _____   6. _____   7. _____
  8. _____   9. _____   10. _____   11. _____   12. _____

実演練習 *Jitsuen renshuu* Performance practice

 1-10-2P Giving a self-introduction

For each situation, say a simple introduction, and listen to how someone might respond. The sample responses use Brian and Sasha, but use your own name when you do your introduction.

Ex. 1.	You are a homestay student introducing yourself to your host mother, Shirai-san.		
You/Brian	ブライアンです。よろしくお願いします。	*Buraian desu. Yoroshiku onegai-shimasu.*	I'm Brian. Nice to meet you.
Host mother	白井です。どうぞよろしく。	*Shirai-desu. Doozo yoroshiku.*	I'm Shirai. Nice to meet you.
Ex. 2.	You are a new student introducing yourself to your teacher, Sakamoto-sensei.		
You/Brian	ブライアン・ワンです。よろしくお願いします。	*Buraian-wan desu. Yoroshiku onegai-shimasu.*	I'm Brian Wang. Nice to meet you.
Teacher	坂本です。どうぞよろしく。	*Sakamoto-desu. Doozo yoroshiku.*	I'm Sakamoto. Nice to meet you.
3.	You are a new employee introducing yourself to your boss, Yagi-san.		
4.	You are a new employee introducing yourself to a co-worker, Ikeda-san.		

1-10 腕試し *Udedameshi* Tryout

Introduce yourself to someone new.

15

理解練習 *Rikai renshuu* Comprehension practice

 1-11-1C What's going on?

Listen to Kanda-san and Sasha, office colleagues, and select from the list the option that best describes the situation. Use each description only once.

Ex. 1. __b__   Ex. 2. __a__   3. __e__   4. __d__   5. __c__

a. Kanda-san is leaving.
b. Sasha is leaving at the end of the workday.
c. Sasha goes off to an appointment.
d. Kanda-san just edited a proposal that Sasha put together for their project.
e. Both Kanda-san and Sasha are leaving the office at the end of the workday.

◆ **Scene 1-12 練習** れんしゅう **Renshuu Practice**

理解練習 りかいれんしゅう ***Rikai renshuu* Comprehension practice**

 1-12-1C What's going on?

Listen to Kanda-san and Sasha, office colleagues, and select from the list the option that best describes the situation. Use each description only once.

Ex. 1. __b__   Ex. 2. __a__   3. _____   4. _____   5. _____

a. Kanda-san returns to the office after attending a meeting elsewhere.
b. Sasha requests that Kanda-san approve a form.
c. Kanda-san gets Sasha's attention.
d. Sasha leaves the office at the end of the workday.
e. Sasha leaves to go to an appointment.

実演練習 じつえんれんしゅう ***Jitsuen renshuu* Performance practice**

1-12-2P Responding to leave-taking (BTS 23)

Respond to each of the leave-taking expressions based on the context.

Ex. 1.	Your host father is leaving for work in the morning.		
Host father	行ってきます。	*Itte kimasu.*	I'm leaving.
You	行ってらっしゃい。	*Itte rasshai.*	See you later.
Ex. 2.	You are leaving your teacher's office after a one-on-one meeting.		
Teacher	じゃあ。	*Jaa.*	Well then.
You	失礼します。	*Shitsuree-shimasu.*	Excuse me.
3.	A co-worker is leaving the office at the end of the day.		
4.	Your project team has finished a big presentation and everybody is going back to their office.		
5.	You and your friends are about to go home after a night out.		

1-12

よろしくお願いします。

17

1-12-3P Leave-taking (BTS 23)

Say a leave-taking expression based on the context and listen to the response.

Ex. 1.	You are leaving for school. Your host family sister is still at home.		
You	行ってきます。	*Itte kimasu.*	I'm leaving.
Host sister	行ってらっしゃい。	*Itte rasshai.*	See you later.
Ex. 2.	You are going home after having spent some time with an elementary school student.		
You	バイバイ。	*Bai bai.*	Bye-bye.
Student	バイバイ。	*Bai bai.*	Bye-bye.
3.	You have been talking to a teacher, and you are leaving her office now.		
4.	You are leaving work, but others are still working.		

よろしくお願いします。 1-12

じつえんれんしゅう
実演練習 *Jitsuen renshuu* **Performance practice**

 1-13-1P Responding to a greeting

Respond to each of the greetings based on the context.

Ex. 1.	You are saying hello to a friend in the morning.		
Friend	おはよう。	*Ohayoo.*	Good morning.
You	おはよう。	*Ohayoo.*	Good morning.
Ex. 2.	You are hiking and pass some other hikers on the hiking trail in the afternoon.		
Hikers	こんにちは。	*Konnichi wa.*	Hello.
You	こんにちは。	*Konnichi wa.*	Hello.
3.	Your host father has just arrived home.		
4.	You are walking past your neighbor who is sweeping the street in front of her house in the morning.		

 1-13-2P Greeting someone

Say a greeting based on the context and listen to the response.

Ex. 1.	You are greeting a senior co-worker as you pass her in the hall.		
You	お疲れ様です。	*Otsukaresama desu.*	Hello.
Senior co-worker	お疲れ様。	*Otsukaresama.*	Hello.
Ex. 2.	You have just arrived home from school. Greet your host mother.		
You	ただいま。	*Tadaima.*	I'm home.
Host mother	おかえり。	*Okaeri.*	Welcome back.
3.	Your co-worker has just returned from her meeting.		
4.	You are exchanging business cards with a new project team member and have just told him your name.		

理解実演練習 *Rikai jitsuen renshuu* Comprehension and performance practice

1-14-1CP Mora count

Listen, repeat, and identify the number of morae (beats) in each item.

Ex. 1. __4__	Ex. 2. __7__	3. _____	4. _____	5. _____
6. _____	7. _____	8. _____	9. _____	10. _____

実演練習 *Jitsuen renshuu* Performance practice

1-14-2P Responding to a greeting

Say a greeting based on the context and listen to the response.

Ex. 1.	You are saying goodnight to a colleague after an evening event.		
You	おやすみなさい。	*Oyasumi nasai.*	Good night.
Host sister	おやすみなさい。	*Oyasumi nasai.*	Good night.
Ex. 2.	You are leaving the office to do some errands.		
You	行<ruby>っ<rt>い</rt></ruby>てきます。	*Itte kimasu.*	I'm leaving.
Neighbor	行<ruby>っ<rt>い</rt></ruby>てらっしゃい。	*Itte rasshai.*	See you later.
3.	You are about to end a meeting with a new client.		
4.	Your colleague is leaving the office for the day, but you still have something to do.		

◆ Scene 1-15 練習 *Renshuu* Practice

読み練習 *Yomi-renshuu* Reading practice

(よ れんしゅう)

1-15-1R Symbol recognition

Underline the kanji in the following. Leave it unmarked if there are no kanji.

Ex. 1. ジョナサン野村

Ex. 2. ブライアンさん、おはよう。(No kanji)

3. 博です。
4. よろしくお願いします。
5. おはよう。
6. 神田さんです。
7. どうも！僕、一郎。
8. ありがとうございました。失礼します。
9. お疲れ様です。
10. 京都駅
11. お帰りなさい。
12. お先に。
13. サーシャ・モリス

1-15-2R Symbol recognition

Underline the katakana in the following.

Ex. 1. 私の家ではテレビはあまり見ません。

Ex. 2. 雨が降りました。(No katakana)

3. 東京ドームに行きました。
4. ミーティング、何時ごろですか。
5. 沖縄のどこ
6. ブライアン・ワンさん
7. じゃあね、バイバイ！
8. サーシャ・モリスです。よろしくお願いします。
9. 行っていらっしゃい。
10. 野菜丸ごとヤサイクル
11. ゴミを減らしてＣＯ２を削減する。
12. いろんな味で食べるエコ。

◆ 評価 *Hyooka* **Assessment**

Answer sheet templates are provided in Appendix B for the Assessment sections.

聞いてみよう *Kiite miyoo* **Listening comprehension**

For each of the following, read the context, listen to the audio, and then answer the questions. The audio may include unfamiliar expressions. If you hear something unfamiliar, rely on what you know to choose the correct answer.

1. Two people greet each other on campus.

   a. What is the relationship between the speakers?
   b. What is the man's name?

2. Two people are at the train station.

   a. What is the relationship between the speakers?
   b. What are they doing?

3. Two people are talking to each other in front of an office building.

   a. When is this conversation taking place?
   b. Who is more senior, the woman or the man?

4. Two people are talking to each other in front of an office building.

   a. Who is staying back?

5. Two people are bowing to each other in an office.

   a. How well do they know each other?
   b. What is the woman's name?
   c. What is the man's name?

6. Two people are bowing to each other at a reception.

   a. What do both speakers express to each other?
   b. What is the woman's name?

使ってみよう *Tsukatte miyoo* **Dry run**

For each of the following, listen to the audio, and respond to what was said based on the context.

1. Your host father is leaving for work.
2. A friend is giving you a pen to borrow.
3. You are passing a friend of yours in the hallway at school in the morning.
4. You respond to a co-worker who is asking for a copy of the new schedule.
5. You are meeting one of the new part-time student workers at the company where you work. (Use your own name in your response. In the sample response, the name Susan Smith will be used.)
6. You are passing a co-worker in the hall.
7. A co-worker is leaving work at the end of the day.
8. You have been visiting your friend's house for dinner. You are now leaving and your friend's mother is speaking to you.
9. Your host mother has returned home from work.

Now it's your turn to start the conversation based on the given context. Listen to how the other person reacts to you. For some items, you may not get a verbal response. If you hear something unfamiliar, rely on what you know to choose the correct answer.

10. You are greeting the other employees when you arrive at the office in the morning.
11. Your boss has been on a business trip the past few days. He has just returned to the office.
12. You sit down next to a friend in class in the morning. It is the first time you've seen your friend today.
13. You and a classmate are both trying to go through the door to class at the same time. Invite your classmate to go first.
14. You are about to finish meeting one of your superiors at work for the first time.
15. You are visiting a teacher in her office in the afternoon.
16. A cashier is asking if you would like your receipt. You would like the receipt.
17. You are passing a teacher in the hall in the afternoon.
18. You are leaving work at the end of the day.
19. You are just about to eat dinner with your host family. Your host mother made the dinner.
20. You are meeting some friends from school for dinner in the evening.

知ってる? *Shitte'ru?* What do you know?

Select the most appropriate option and write the letter in the space on your answer sheet.

1. You would say はい *Hai* when you _____. (BTS 1)

   a. thank someone for something he did
   b. ask someone to do something for you
   c. hand something over to someone

Act 1

よろしくお願いします。

2. ～さん, ～先生^{せんせい}, and ～くん (*~san, ~sensei, and ~kun*) are not attached to your _____ name. (BTS 2)

    a. co-worker's
    (b.) own
    c. teacher's

3. What is the conventional order of names in Japanese? (BTS 2)

    (a.) Surname then the given name
    b. Given name then surname

4. Sometimes ～さん *~san* is dropped after someone's name. Who is more likely to do so? (BTS 2)

    a. A host to a guest
    b. An assistant to a supervisor
    (c.) A manager to an assistant

5. You want to thank your teacher for her signature on a form. What would you say? (BTS 4)

    a. ありがとう。*Arigatoo.*
    (b.) ありがとうございました。*Arigatoo gozaimashita.*
    c. お願^{ねが}いします。*Onegai shimasu.*

6. You want to preface your request with an apology. (BTS 5)

    (a.) すみません。*Sumimasen.*
    b. お願^{ねが}いします。*Onegai shimasu.*
    c. 失礼^{しつれい}しました。*Shitsurei shimashita.*

7. You've just introduced yourself by name to the new intern. What else could you add? (BTS 9)

    a. どうもありがとう。*Doomo arigatoo.*
    b. こちらこそ。*Kochira koso.*
    (c.) よろしくお願^{ねが}いします。*Yoroshiku onegai shimasu.*

8. Upon entering the teacher's office, you would say _____. (BTS 11)

    a. お願^{ねが}いします。*Onegai shimasu.*
    b. お先^{さき}に失礼^{しつれい}します。*Osaki ni shitsurei shimasu.*
    (c.) 失礼^{しつれい}します。*Shitsurei shimasu.*

9. It's 9:00 a.m. and you greet your new host family's father. What would you say? (BTS 12)

    a. おはよう。*Ohayoo.*
    (b.) おはようございます。*Ohayoo gozaimasu.*
    c. こんにちは。*Konnichi wa.*

よろしくお願いします。

10. It's 9:00 a.m. and you leave your homestay for school. What would you say to your host mother? (BTS 17)

    a. そようなら。*Sayoonara.*
    b. バイバイ。*Bai bai.*
    c. 行ってきます。*Itte kimasu.*

11. You say goodbye to your best friend after school. (BTS 18)

    a. では、失礼します。*De wa, shitsurei shimasu.*
    b. さよなら。*Sayonara.*
    c. じゃね、また。*Ja ne, mata.*

12. You greet your roommate who has just come home. What would you say? (BTS 17)

    a. 行ってらっしゃい。*Itte rasshai.*
    b. お帰りなさい。*Okaerinasai.*
    c. ただいま。*Tadaima.*

13. You're being introduced to the mayor of the town. How would you refer to yourself in your introduction? (BTS 15)

    a. 僕 *Boku*
    b. あたし *Atashi*
    c. 私 *Watakushi*

14. You're about to start eating dinner with your friend. What would you say? (BTS 13)

    a. いただきます。*Itadakimasu.*
    b. どうぞ。*Doozo.*
    c. ご馳走様でした。*Gochisoosama deshita.*

15. You're finishing a meal with your co-worker. What would you say? (BTS 13)

    a. お疲れ様でした。*Otsukaresama deshita.*
    b. ご馳走様でした。*Gochisoosama deshita.*
    c. 失礼しました。*Shitsurei shimashita*

16. You've come to the end of a workshop and want to thank everyone for their work. What would you say? (BTS 22)

    a. では、また。*De wa, mata.*
    b. 失礼しました。*Shitsurei shimashita.*
    c. お疲れ様でした。*Otsukaresama deshita.*

17. Each kana symbol represents a _____. (BTL 1)

    a. word
    b. sound
    c. mora

25

Act 1　よろしくお願いします。

18. Kanji were originally borrowed from _____. (BTL 2)

    a. China
    b. Korea
    c. Nepal

19. 縦書き *Tategaki* refers to script that is written _____. (BTL 3)

    a. left to right, horizontally
    b. right to left, vertically
    c. left to right, vertically

20. Furigana is also called _____. (BTL 4)

    a. *rubi*
    b. *kanji*
    c. *ten-ten*

21. 振仮名 Furigana refers to kana that _____. (BTL 4)

    a. assists readers with pronunciation
    b. substitutes for kanji in *tategaki*
    c. helps people to write kanji

22. 原稿用紙 *Genkooyooshi* refers to _____. (BTL 5)

    a. small squares for writing kanji
    b. writing assignments
    c. special paper for writing Japanese

だいじょう ぶ
大丈夫です。

Daijoobu desu.

It'll be fine.

せん り　　　　みち　　いっぽ
千里の道も一歩から　*Senri no michi mo ippo kara*
A journey of a thousand miles begins
with a single step.

◆ **Scene 2-0** 練習 れんしゅう *Renshuu* **Practice**

理解練習 り かいれんしゅう *Rikai renshuu* **Comprehension practice**

2-0-1C Responding to instructional expressions

Listen and select from the illustrations the appropriate response to each instructional expression.

Ex. 1. _d_   Ex. 2. _c_   3. _b_   4. _e_   5. _g_

6. _f_   7. _a_   8. _d_   9. _h_   10. _b_

11. _d_   12. _f_   13. _c_   14. _g_   15. _a_

16. _c_   17. _e_   18. _b_   19. _g_   20. _h_

2-0-2C Responding appropriately

Listen to the audio and select the most appropriate response to the command.

Ex. 1. __c__   Ex. 2. __a__   3. _____   4. _____   5. _____

6. _____   7. _____   8. _____   9. _____

Ex. 1.

    a. Tell Jones-san the answer one more time.
    b. Ask Jones-san a question.
    c. Say it to Jones-san.
    d. Repeat what Jones-san said.

Ex. 2.

    a. Read something.
    b. Ask a question.
    c. Listen to the teacher.
    d. Close your book.

3.

    a. Respond to what was said.
    b. Ask a question.
    c. Stop using any language other than Japanese.
    d. Put your phone away.

4.

    a. Tell Chen-san the answer.
    b. Ask Chen-san a question.
    c. Say it to Chen-san again.
    d. Listen.

5.

    a. Stop using any language other than Japanese.
    b. Respond when it's your turn.
    c. Say it together with the rest of the class.
    d. Close your book.

6.

    a. Put your phone away.
    b. Respond to what was said.
    c. Listen.
    d. Say it louder.

だいじょうぶ
大丈夫です。

7.

a. Listen.
b. Look at something.
c. Say it again.
d. Put your phone away.

8.

a. Ask Smith-san one more time.
b. Repeat what Smith-san said.
c. Tell Smith-san the answer.
d. Say it to Smith-san.

9.

a. Repeat what Wilson-san said.
b. Ask Wilson-san one more time.
c. Say "Wilson-san" more clearly.
d. Give the answer to Wilson-san.

 ## 2-0-3C What's going on?

Listen to each conversation and select from the list the description that best tells what the man is doing. Use each description only once.

Ex. 1. __c__   Ex. 2. __d__   3. _____   4. _____   5. _____

6. _____   7. _____

a. Reading a name.
b. Thanking for something he received.
c. Agreeing to speak in Japanese.
d. Bidding farewell.
e. Greeting his subordinate.
f. Making a request to a new acquaintance.
g. Beginning a meal.

◆ Scene 2-1 練習 *Renshuu* Practice

理解練習 *Rikai renshuu* Comprehension practice

 2-1-1C Yes or no? (BTS 1)

Listen to each statement and select from the list the English that corresponds to what the speaker says.

Ex. 1. __a__   Ex. 2. __b__   3. _____   4. _____   5. _____

6. _____   7. _____   8. _____   9. _____   10. _____

Ex. 1.   a. I'll do it.
         b. I won't do it.

Ex. 2.   a. I understand it.
         b. I don't understand it.

3.   a. I can do this.
     b. I can't do this.

4.   a. I'll do my best.
     b. I'll go easy.

5.   a. It's that one that we both know about.
     b. It's not that one that we both know about.

6.   a. I'm all right.
     b. I'm not all right.

7.   a. My choice is that one close to you.
     b. My choice is not that one close to you.

8.   a. It's me.
     b. It's not me.

9.   a. That is awesome.
     b. That's not a big deal.

10. a. It's fine.
     b. It's not fine.

実演練習 *Jitsuen renshuu* Performance practice

2-1-2P Affirming and negating (BTS 1, 2, 5)

Respond to Yagi-san's question based on the illustrations. If Yagi-san is correct, respond affirmatively. If Yagi-san is incorrect, use the negative form じゃないです *ja nai desu* in your response. Remember that Yagi-san will refer to something that you have with それ *sore*, but you will refer to the same item with これ *kore,* and vice-versa.

Ex. 1.

| Yagi-san | それですか。 | *Sore desu ka?* | Is it that one? |
| You | はい、これです。 | *Hai, kore desu.* | Yes, it's this one. |

Ex. 2.

| Yagi-san | あれですか。 | *Are desu ka?* | Is it that one over there? |
| You | いえ、あれじゃないです。 | *Ie, are ja nai desu.* | No, it's not that one over there. |

3.

4.

32

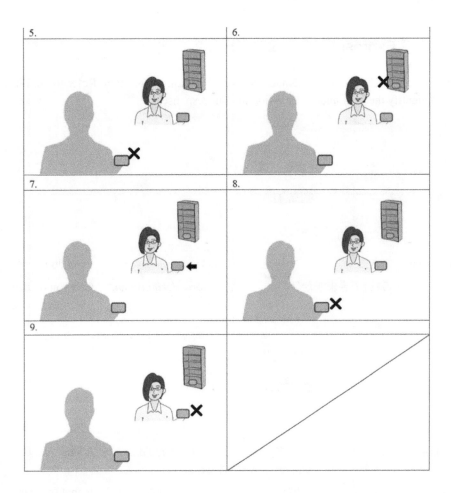

 2-1-3P Refuting an idea (BTS 1, 5)

Let Tanaka-san know that her assumption is incorrect.

Ex. 1.

Tanaka-san	わかりますか？	*Wakarimasu ka?*	Do they understand?
You	いえ、わかりません。	*Ie, wakarimasen.*	No, they don't.

Ex. 2.

Tanaka-san	先生ですか？	*Sensee desu ka?*	Is she a teacher?
You	いえ、先生じゃありません。	*Ie, sensee ja arimasen.*	No, she isn't.

2-1-4P Expressing doubt (BTS 1, 2, 3, 4)

Express your doubt about what Kanda-san says by asking a question. Refer to the illustration to identify the item under discussion in your response.

Ex. 1.

Kanda-san	できます。	*Dekimasu.*	I can do it.
You	これ、できますか?	*Kore, dekimasu ka?*	Can you do this (near me)?

Ex. 2.

Kanda-san	大丈夫じゃないです。	*Daijoobu ja nai desu.*	It's not okay.
You	あれ、大丈夫じゃないですか?	*Are, daijoobu ja nai desu ka?*	Is that (over there) not okay?

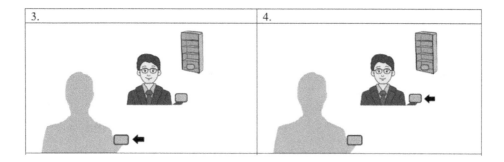

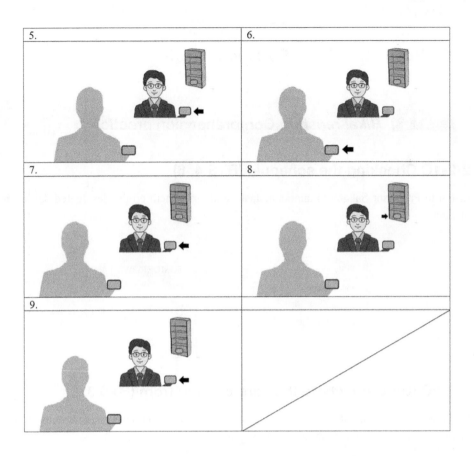

♦ Scene 2-2 練習 *Renshuu* Practice

理解練習 *Rikai renshuu* Comprehension practice

 2-2-1C Checking the schedule (BTS 4, 6)

Listen to Professor Sakamoto announce tasks and write them on the designated day in the planner.

TODAY
• Homework
• Test
• Meeting

TOMORROW
• Phone call
• HW
•
•

 2-2-2C Knowing where they are coming from (BTS 3, 6)

Circle a, b, or c to identify whether the speaker is (a) asking a question; (b) seeking confirmation; (c) telling you something new or significant.

Ex. 1. a / (b) / c   Ex. 2. a / b / (c)   3. (a) / b / c   4. a / b (c)

5. a (b) c   6. (a) b / c   7. a (b) c   8. (a) b / c

9. a / b (c)   10. (a) b / c   11. a (b) c   12. (a) b / c

実演練習 *Jitsuen renshuu* Performance practice

 2-2-3P Providing correction (BTS 1, 3, 6, 14)

Your colleague Murata-san is checking on things with you. Respond "no" to his questions. If he asks an affirmative question, soften your response with *nee*. If he asks a negative question, provide an assertive response with *yo*.

Ex. 1.

Murata-san	わかりますか?	*Wakarimasu ka?*	Do you understand?
You	いえ、わかりませんねえ。	*Ie, wakarimasen nee.*	No, I don't, you know.

Ex. 2.

| Murata-san | しないですか? | *Shinai desu ka?* | Are you not going to do it? |
| You | いえいえ、しますよ。 | *Ieie, shimasu yo.* | No, I will do it. |

2-2-4P Correcting a misconception (BTS 7, 8, 9)

When Kadota-san, a staff member at the international student office, assumes you'll do a task, react with surprise asking if he means for YOU (to do it) and check the timeline he mentions. Politely, and hesitantly, tell him you can't. Then apologize.

Ex. 1.

| Kadota-san | レポート、今日書きま
すね? | *Repooto, kyoo kakimasu ne?* | You are going to write the report, today, right? |
| You | あのう、私ですか?
今日ですか?ええと、い
え、ちょっと……。すみ
ません。 | *Anoo, watashi desu ka? Kyoo desu ka? Eeto, ie, chotto . . . Sumimasen.* | Umm, you mean, me? Today? Umm, it's not possible. Sorry. |

Ex. 2.

| Kadota-san | 今、テスト始めますね? | *Ima, tesuto hajimemasu ne?* | You are going to start the test now right? |
| You | あのう、私ですか? 今
ですか? ええと、いえ、
ちょっと……。すみま
せん。 | *Anoo, watashi desu ka? Ima desu ka? Eeto, ie, chotto . . . Sumimasen.* | Umm, you mean, me? Now? Umm, it's not possible. Sorry. |

2-2 腕試し *Udedameshi* Tryout

Observe Japanese people talking to each other, and listen for *chotto*. You can observe people around you, or watch Japanese television shows or movies that use live actors. What did *chotto* mean when each speaker used it?

◆ Scene 2-3 練習 *Renshuu* Practice

理解練習 *Rikai renshuu* Comprehension practice

2-3-1C What's being offered? (BTS 10)

Listen to each conversation and select the food or beverage that is being offered.

Ex. 1. __b__   Ex. 2. __e__   3. _____   4. _____   5. _____

6. _____   7. _____   8. _____   9. _____   10. _____

a. breakfast	b. udon	c. ramen	d. cake	e. curry rice
f. soba	g. coffee	h. tea	i. boxed meal	j. water
k. milk	l. beer	m. juice		

2-3-2C Accepted or declined? (BTS 11, 12)

Listen to each conversation and write A if the invitation is accepted and D if it is declined.

Ex. 1. __a__   Ex. 2. __d__   3. _____   4. _____   5. _____

6. _____   7. _____   8. _____   9. _____   10. _____

理解実演練習 *Rikai jitsuen renshuu*
Comprehension and performance practice

2-3-3CP Inviting a colleague (BTS 11)

Based on the illustration, invite a colleague to have some food/beverage or engage in an activity. Then listen to the model and the response and mark each item as accepted (☺) or declined (☹).

Ex. 1.

You	クッキー、よかったら食べませんか？	*Kukkii, yokattara tabemasen ka?*	Won't you have some cookies, if you'd like?
Colleague	あ、いただきます。おいしそうですね。	*A, itadakimasu. Oishisoo desu ne.*	Thank you. I'll take some. They look delicious.

Ex. 2.

You	烏龍茶、よかったら飲みませんか？	*Uuroncha, yokattara nomimasen ka?*	Won't you have some Oolong tea, if you'd like?
Colleague	あ、今いいです。どうも。	*A, ima ii desu. Doo mo.*	Oh, I'm okay now. Thanks.

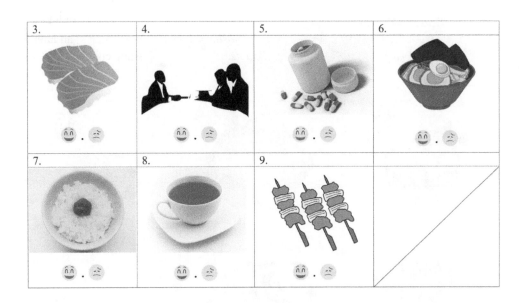

実演練習 *Jitsuen renshuu* **Performance practice**

🎧 2-3-4P Expressing agreement (BTS 14, 15)

Yoshida-san, a co-worker, comments about the items in the illustrations. Express your agreement, mentioning the item in your response.

Ex. 1.

Yoshida-san	すごいですねぇ。	*Sugoi desu nee.*	(That's) amazing!
You	ええ、すごいケーキで すねぇ。	*Ee, sugoi keeki desu nee.*	Yeah, (that's) an amaz- ing cake!

Ex. 2.

Yoshida-san	面白いですねぇ。	*Omoshiroi desu nee.*	(That's) interesting!
You	ええ、面白いクッキーで すねぇ。	*Ee, omoshiroi kukkii desu nee.*	Yeah, (that's) an inter- esting cookie!

40

2-3 腕試し *Udedameshi* Tryout

1. Try inviting your Japanese associates to partake in food and activities that may be enjoyable for them.
2. Try offering some food items to share with your Japanese colleagues, classmates, and other acquaintances. See if they use the name of the item in their echo questions.
3. Ask a Japanese friend or associate if she likes various kinds of food.

◆ Scene 2-4 練習 *Renshuu* Practice

実演練習 *Jitsuen renshuu* Performance practice

 2-4-1P Leaving it open-ended (BTS 16)

Your associate asks you to confirm an assumption. Agree while suggesting there is more to the story.

Ex. 1.

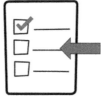

| Tanaka-san | これ、今しますね？ | *Kore, ima shimasu ne?* | You are going to do this now, right? |
| You | しますけど・・・・・。 | *Shimasu kedo . . .* | Yes, but (why do you ask?) |

Ex. 2.

| Tanaka-san | あした、忙しいですね？ | *Ashita, isogashii desu ne?* | You are busy tomorrow, right? |
| You | 忙しいですけど・・・・・。 | *Isogashii desu kedo. . . .* | Yes, I am, but (why do you ask?) |

◆ Scene 2-5 練習 *Renshuu* Practice

理解練習 *Rikai renshuu* Comprehension practice

2-5-1C What's going on? (BTS 7, 16, 17)

In each exchange, you will hear a word from the こちら *kochira*, そちら *sochira*, あちら *achira*, どちら *dochira* series. Circle what the word refers to. If you hear something unfamiliar, rely on what you know to choose the correct answer.

Ex. 1.	a) location	(b) object	c) person
Ex. 2.	(a) location	b) object	c) person
3.	a) location	b) object	c) person
4.	a) location	b) object	c) person
5.	a) location	b) object	c) person

2-5-2C Asking or stating? (BTS 18)

Listen to what the man says and circle the type of utterance you hear.

Ex. 1. Question /(Statement)   Ex. 2.(Question)/ Statement   3. Question / Statement

4. Question / Statement   5. Question / Statement   6. Question / Statement

7. Question / Statement   8. Question / Statement   9. Question / Statement

2-5-3C Acknowledgment or disbelief? (BTS 19)

Listen to how Sasha responds to Murata-san, her co-worker. Then mark the happy face if Sasha simply acknowledges what he said, or the surprised face if she expresses some surprise or disbelief. If you hear something unfamiliar, rely on what you know to choose the correct answer.

Ex. 1.

Ex. 2.

3.

4.

5.

6.

実演練習 *Jitsuen renshuu* Performance practice
<ruby>じつえんれんしゅう</ruby>

🎧 **2-5-4P Responding to new information (BTS 19)**

Respond to your colleague with *Soo desu ka.* (acknowledgment) or *Soo desu ka?* (disbelief), according to the illustrations.

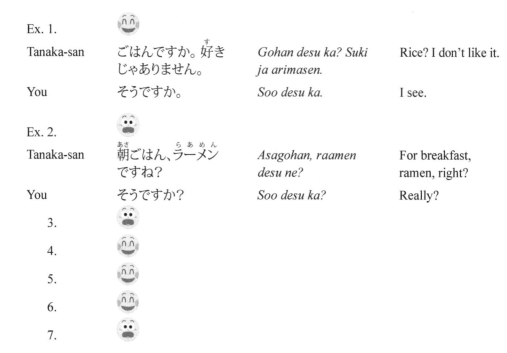

Ex. 1.			
Tanaka-san	ごはんですか。好き じゃありません。	*Gohan desu ka? Suki ja arimasen.*	Rice? I don't like it.
You	そうですか。	*Soo desu ka.*	I see.

Ex. 2.			
Tanaka-san	朝ごはん、ラーメン ですね?	*Asagohan, raamen desu ne?*	For breakfast, ramen, right?
You	そうですか?	*Soo desu ka?*	Really?

3.

4.

5.

6.

7.

2-5 腕試し *Udedameshi* Tryout
<ruby>うでだめ</ruby>

Call your Japanese colleagues, classmates, and other acquaintances on their cell phones. Pay attention to what they say when they answer the phone.

44

◆ Scene 2-6 練習 *Renshuu* Practice

理解練習 *Rikai renshuu* Comprehension practice

 2-6-1C What's going on? (BTS 25)

Listen to what your neighbor, Shirai-san, says and circle what she concludes. If you hear something unfamiliar, rely on what you know to choose the correct answer.

Ex. 1.

    a. Shirai-san is familiar with what is being talked about.

    (b.) Shirai-san doesn't know what is being talked about.

Ex. 2.

    (a.) Everything is fine.

    b. There is a problem.

3.

    a. Shirai-san will go tomorrow.

    b. Shirai-san won't go tomorrow.

4.

    a. It's amazing.

    b. It's not very impressive.

5.

    a. The person is a teacher.

    b. The person is not a teacher.

6.

    a. It's a good idea.

    b. It's not a very good idea.

7.

    a. Shirai-san likes it.

    b. Shirai-san doesn't like it.

8.

    a. Shirai-san can do it.

    b. Shirai-san can't do it.

2-6 大丈夫です。

9.

    a. It tastes good.

    b. It doesn't taste good.

10.

    a. Everything is fine.

    b. There is a problem.

11.

    a. It's going to be Shirai-san.

    b. It is not going to be Shirai-san.

 ## 2-6-2C What's the style? (BTS 25)

Listen to what your neighbor, Shirai-san, says and circle the style she uses. If you hear something unfamiliar, rely on what you know to choose the correct answer.

Ex. 1.	a) formal	**b) informal**
Ex. 2.	**a) formal**	b) informal
3.	a) formal	**b) informal**
4.	**a) formal**	b) informal
5.	a) formal	**b) informal**
6.	a) formal	**b) informal**
7.	a) formal	**b) informal**
8.	**a) formal**	b) informal
9.	**a) formal**	b) informal

実演練習 じつえんれんしゅう *Jitsuen renshuu* **Performance practice**

 ## 2-6-3P Expressing uncertainty (BTS 17, 22, 23, 24)

When a colleague, Uchida-san, asks you to identify someone or something, make a comment to yourself before responding that you are unsure. Be careful not to look at Uchida-san when making the self-directed comment.

Ex. 1.

Uchida-san	あちらは？ 寺田さん てらだ ですか？	*Achira wa? Terada- san desu ka?*	What about that (one) over there? Is it Terada-san?

You	さあ、だれかなあ…… わかりませんねぇ。	*Saa, dare ka naa . . .* *Wakarimasen nee.*	Hmmm, I wonder who. . . . I'm not sure.
Ex. 2.			
Uchida-san	そちらは？　お茶です か？	*Sochira wa? Ocha* *desu ka?*	What about that (one) over there? Is it tea?
You	さあ、何かなあ…… わかりませんねぇ。	*Saa, nani ka naa . . .* *Wakarimasen nee.*	Hmmm, I wonder what. . . . I'm not sure.

2-6-4P Expressing uncertainty (BTS 23, 24, 25)

When a colleague, Tomoda-san, asks you about what Murata-san is going to do, make a comment to yourself before responding that you are unsure. Be careful not to look at Tomoda-san when making the self-directed comment.

Ex. 1.			
Tomoda-san	村田さん、来ます かね。	*Murata-san, kimasu* *kane.*	I wonder if Murata- san will come.
You	来ないかな。ちょっと わかりませんねぇ。	*Konai kana. Chotto* *wakarimasen nee.*	I wonder if he won't. I'm not sure.
Ex. 2.			
Tomoda-san	村田さん、飲みます かね。	*Murata-san, nomi-* *masu kane.*	I wonder if Murata- san will drink.
You	飲まないかな。ちょっ とわかりませんねぇ。	*Nomanai kana. Chotto* *wakarimasen nee.*	I wonder if he won't. I'm not sure.

2-6 腕試し *Udedameshi* Tryout

1. Using a Japanese newspaper (if using an online newspaper, such as *Yomiuri* or *Asahi*, be sure the website is displayed in Japanese!), ask the names of people whose pictures appear in the newspaper. Use an echo question to confirm the accuracy of your pronunciation.
2. Listen in on some conversations that occur between Japanese people around you to see if you can tell what titles are being used to address or refer to some of them.

理解練習 *Rikai renshuu* Comprehension practice

2-7-1C Where is it? (BTS 28)

Listen to Amy ask Takashi the location of an item. Then circle where the item is. If you hear something unfamiliar, rely on what you know to choose the correct answer.

Ex. 1.	(a) by Takashi	b) by Amy	c) away from both of them
Ex. 2.	a) by Takashi	b) by Amy	(c) away from both of them
3.	a) by Takashi	(b) by Amy	c) away from both of them
4.	(a) by Takashi	b) by Amy	c) away from both of them
5.	a) by Takashi	b) by Amy	(c) away from both of them
6.	a) by Takashi	(b) by Amy	c) away from both of them
7.	(a) by Takashi	b) by Amy	c) away from both of them

実演練習 *Jitsuen renshuu* Performance practice

2-7-2P Answering questions

Respond to your colleague Murata-san's assumptions based on the illustrations. Use ええ *ee* to indicate your agreement, and そうですか？ *soo desu ka?* to indicate your disagreement.

Ex. 1.

| Murata-san | おいしそうじゃないですね。 | *Oishisoo ja nai desu ne.* | It doesn't look appetizing. |

| You | お弁当ですか？ええ、おいしそうじゃないですね。 | *Obentoo desu ka? Ee, oishisoo ja nai desu ne.* | This lunch box? Right, it doesn't look delicious, does it. |

Ex. 2.

| Murata-san | 遠くないですね。 | *Tooku nai desu ne.* | It's not far, is it? |
| You | 会社ですか？そうですか？遠いですよ。 | *Kaisha desu ka? Soo desu ka? Tooi desu yo.* | The company? Really? (I disagree) It's far, you know. |

2-7-3P Refuting an idea (BTS 23)

Tanaka-san asks you for your opinion. Assume your response is bad news, and use Particle
ねぇ *nee* to soften your response.

Ex. 1.

| Tanaka-san | 近いですか？ | *Chikai desu ka?* | Is it close? |
| You | いえ、近くないですねぇ。 | *Ie, chikaku nai desu nee.* | No, it's not close. |

Ex. 2.

| Tanaka-san | 美味しそうですか？ | *Oishisoo desu ka?* | Does it look tasty? |
| You | いえ、美味しそうじゃない
ですねぇ。 | *Ie, oishisoo ja nai desu
nee.* | No, it doesn't look tasty. |

◆ Scene 2-8 練習 (れんしゅう) *Renshuu* Practice

理解練習 (りかいれんしゅう) *Rikai renshuu* Comprehension practice

 2-8-1C What's going on? (BTS 29)

Listen to each statement and select the option (a or b) that corresponds to what the speaker says.

Ex. 1.   (a.) It isn't tea.
           b. I don't have any tea.

Ex. 2.   a. Isn't that a cell phone?
          (b.) Do you not have a cell phone?

3.   a. No, it's not ramen.
       b. No, I don't have any ramen.

4.   a. It isn't beer.
       b. I don't have any beer.

5.   a. It's not homework.
       b. I don't have any homework.

実演練習 (じつえんれんしゅう) *Jitsuen renshuu* Performance practice

 2-8-2P Checking on what's being asked (BTS 29)

Listen to your colleague's question and respond based on the illustration.

Ex. 1.

| Colleague | コーヒー (こおひい) ですか? | *Koohii desu ka?* | Is (that) coffee? |
| You | これですか? はい、コーヒー (こおひい) ですよ。 | *Kore desu ka? Hai, koohii desu yo.* | (You mean) this? Yes, it's coffee. |

51

Ex. 2.

| Colleague | コーヒー、ありますか？ | *Koohii arimasu ka?* | Do you have coffee? |
| You | コーヒーですか？　はい、ありますよ。 | *Koohii desu ka? Hai, arimasu yo.* | Coffee? Yes, we have (some). |

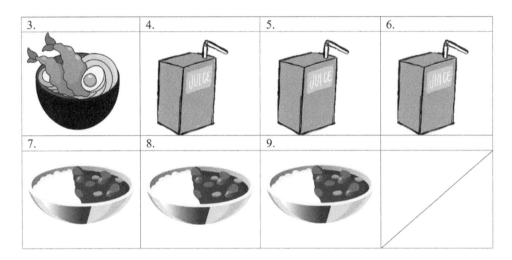

読み練習 ^よ^{れんしゅう} *Yomi-renshuu* Reading practice

2-9-1R Identifying things and people

Identify where the thing or person is in relation to the writer.

a. Near the writer
b. Near the addressee
c. Away from the writer and the other person
d. Not sure

Ex. 1. これです。	a
Ex. 2. それです。	b
3. これですか。	_____
4. あれですか。	_____
5. どれですか。	_____
6. あ、あれですか。	_____
7. あれ、だれですか。	_____
8. どれですか。これですか。	_____

2-9-2R Asking various questions

Indicate whether the following questions are yes/no questions or wh-questions (questions that require more than yes or no).

Ex. 1. これ、どうですか。	Yes/no	(Wh)
Ex. 2. あれ、高い^{たか}ですか。	(Yes/no)	Wh
3. 仕事^{しごと}、ありませんか。	Yes/no	Wh
4. 寺田^{てらだ}さん、どちらですか。	Yes/no	Wh

2-9 大丈夫です。

53

5. 神田さん、そちらですか。   Yes/no   Wh

6. 先生、今、お宅ですか。   Yes/no   Wh

7. 坂田さん、行きませんか。   Yes/no   Wh

8. 赤坂さん、今忙しいですか。   Yes/no   Wh

書き練習 *Kaki-renshuu* Writing practice

文字練習 *Moji renshuu* Symbol practice

Use the Symbol Practice sheets in Appendix A to practice *hiragana* characters #1-24 for Scene 2-9.

2-9-3W Writing furigana

Based on the romanized scripts, write the furigana for the following names on the guest list. Remember, names written in Japanese start with the last name followed by the first name, which is the opposite of the Western order that appears in the romanized scripts.

ゲストリスト

Ex. 1. 安西　義男
Yoshio Anzai

4. 須田　友恵
Tomoe Suda

Ex. 2. 立石　空
Sora Tateishi

5. 有山　斗真
Tooma Ariyama

3. 金子　良樹
Yoshiki Kaneko

6. 福地　怜
Rei Fukuchi

54

2-9

大丈夫です。

◆ 評価 *Hyooka* Assessment

Answer sheet templates are provided in Appendix B for the Assessment sections.

聞いてみよう *Kiite miyoo* Listening comprehension

Read the context, listen to the audio, and then answer the questions. If you hear something unfamiliar, rely on what you know to choose the correct answer.

1. Class just started.

   a. Who is the woman?
   b. What is the most likely reason that Wang-san is apologizing?

2. Kanda-san is looking at a file in a document case near the Division Chief, Yagi-san's desk.

   a. What does Kanda-san want to do?
   b. Why does Yagi-san apologize?
   c. Why does Kanda-san apologize?

3. Sasha and her work associate have been working hard on a project.

   a. What have they decided to do?
   b. Which of them seems to be primarily in charge of this project?

4. Kanda-san is talking to Sasha on the phone.

   a. What day are they talking about?
   b. Where will Sasha work that day?
   c. How does Kanda-san feel about this?

5. Takashi, a Japanese student at a US college, makes a comment about a task that his friend, Amy, is doing.

   a. What does Takashi think of the task Amy is doing?
   b. What is Amy's response?
   c. Does Takashi agree with Amy?

6. A man just walked into the office of Ogaki Trading.

   a. Who is the man looking for?
   b. What does the woman think the person in question is doing?
   c. How certain is she of this?

7. Kanda-san and Yagi-san are talking to each other.

   a. What item is being discussed?
   b. How does Kanda-san react to what Yagi-san tells him?
   c. What is Yagi-san's response to Kanda-san's reaction?

8. Brian is talking to his homestay mother, Mrs. Shirai.

    a. What does Brian offer to do?
    b. Is the thing Mrs. Shirai refers to near her or near Brian?
    c. Does Mrs. Shirai think the task will be easy or difficult?

9. Takashi is talking to his friend Amy.

    a. Is Takashi's initial question a factual question or an invitation?
    b. How does Amy respond?
    c. What reason does Amy give for her response?

10. Kanda-san and Sasha are walking back from a morning meeting.

    a. What does Kanda-san suggest?
    b. Does Sasha accept or reject the invitation?
    c. What does Sasha suggest?
    d. How does Kanda-san respond to this suggestion?

 使ってみよう *Tsukatte miyoo* Dry run

Listen to Kanda-san's questions and respond based on the context provided.

1. You are able do the job that needs to be done.
2. You don't know any French.
3. You think the new poster is amazing.
4. You are fluent in English.
5. The new equipment is quite difficult to operate.
6. The train station is not far away.
7. It's oolong tea, not black tea.
8. There is juice.

Now it's your turn to start the conversation based on the given context. Listen to how the other person reacts to you. For some items, you may not get a verbal response. If you hear something unfamiliar, rely on what you know to choose the correct answer.

9. You are attending a reception. There is a large selection of delicious food. Tell your colleague that it looks delicious.
10. Ask your colleague what she'll have for (a) lunch; (b) dinner.
11. Ask a senior student if there isn't (a) homework; (b) a convenience store; (c) a restroom.
12. You and your colleague are trying to decide what to have for dinner. Ask if he likes (a) curry rice; (b) yakitori; (c) sushi; (d) soba noodles.
13. Ask your colleague if there is anything to be done.
14. Ask your colleague which of the two containers holds (a) milk; (b) dinner; (c) homework assignments; (d) reports; (e) cell phones.

15. Assuming that the junior student knows what you are talking about, invite him to
(a) write it; (b) start it; (c) do it; (d) end it; (e) do his best; (f) go there; (g) read it.

読んでみよう *Yonde miyoo* Contextualized reading

In the following exercises you will encounter various texts that are used in contemporary Japanese society, along with a description of the context and other relevant information. By 'text' here we mean any printed work, whether it is a book, a newspaper, an academic paper, an advertisement, or an email.

In any culture you are likely to see a multitude of texts and text types. Some (handwritten notes, text messages, and emails) are short and to the point, especially when the reader and writer know each other well. Such short messages can be similar in style to spoken language. Later we will contrast these short texts with longer, more complex texts that you are likely to come across in Japanese.

Handwritten memos

1. Iida-san, your coworker, borrowed your folder yesterday. Today you find this handwritten sticky note on the folder.

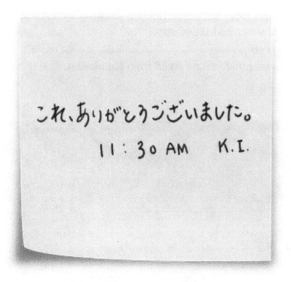

a. What is the purpose of this note?

2. The other day, you gave Terada-san, your acquaintance, some homemade sweets in a plastic container. Today you received a handwritten note on the empty container from Terada-san.

a. What is the purpose of this note?

Text messages

The following examples assume you are reading the texts with some help from a furigana-generating website, browser add-on, or app.

1. Here is a text message that you received from Kanda-san.

a. What does the sender want to know?

2. Here is another text message you received from Kanda-san.

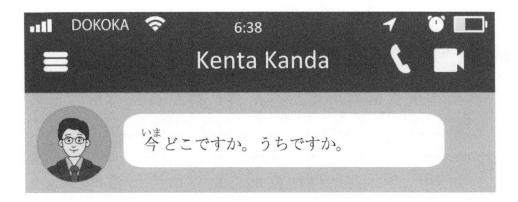

今どこですか。うちですか。

   a. What does the sender want to know?

3. You sent your new friend a photo of a dish at a new restaurant. He responds:

ありがとうございます！

おいしそうですね。高いですか？

a. How does your friend react to the photo?

b. What does he ask?

 書き取り *Kakitori* Dictation

Listen, imagine the context, repeat silently what you hear, then write it down.

1. _____。

2. _____。

3. _____。

4. _____。

5. _____。

6. _____。

7. _____。

8. _____。

書いてみよう *Kaite miyoo* Contextualized writing

Consider the context provided and write a note according to the directions.

1. You are returning a book you borrowed from your colleague. On a sticky note attached to the book, write a thank-you memo.

2. You have found a folder your colleague was looking for. Leave it on his desk with a sticky note asking if this is it.

知ってる? *Shitte'ru?* What do you know?

Select the most appropriate option and write the letter in the space on your answer sheet.

1. You ask if there's a particular item on the menu. (BTS 4, 29)
   すみません。＿＿＿＿＿ありますか。*Sumimasen. ＿＿＿＿＿ arimasu ka.*

   a. ケーキ *Keeki*
   b. どこ *Doko*
   c. おいしい *Oishii*

2. You warn your co-worker about an upcoming event. (BTS 1)
   ＿＿＿＿＿＿＿ないですよ。＿＿＿＿＿＿ *nai desu yo.*

   a. おもしろそう *Omoshirosoo*
   b. おもしろく *Omoshiroku*
   c. つまらない *Tsumaranai*

3. You have some doubt about whether something is okay. (BTS 3, 6, 24)
   いい＿＿＿＿＿ *Ii ＿＿＿＿＿*

   a. ね! *ne!*
   b. よ。*yo.*
   c. かなあ。*ka naa.*

4. You don't understand something that's right in front of you. (BTS 2)
   ＿＿＿＿＿わかりませんねえ。＿＿＿＿ *wakarimasen nee.*

   a. これ*Kore*
   b. それ *Sore*
   c. あれ *Are*

5. You think something looks delicious. (Scene 2-3)
   ＿＿＿＿＿＿＿ですねえ。＿＿＿＿＿*desu nee.*

a. おいしい *Oishii*

b. おいしそう *Oishisoo*

c. おもしろい *Omoshiroi*

6. You disagree with someone's opinion. (BTS 1)

いや、＿＿＿＿＿＿じゃないですよ。 *Iya, ＿＿＿＿＿＿ja nai desu yo.*

a. 高^{たか}く *takaku*

b. きれい *kiree*

c. しません *shimasen*

7. You want to clarify what someone else is talking about. (BTS 7)

今日^{きょう}＿＿＿＿＿＿ *Kyoo ＿＿＿＿＿＿*

a. ですか。 *desu ka.*

b. は？ *wa?*

c. ですよ。 *desu yo.*

8. You're reluctant to comply with a request. (BTS 9)

a. できません。 *Dekimasen.*

b. わかりません。 *Wakarimasen.*

c. ちょっと。 *Chotto.*

9. You've just been complimented by your co-worker. You respond: (BTS 5)

a. いえいえ。 *Ieie.*

b. ちょっと。 *Chotto.*

c. そうですね！ *Soo desu ne!*

10. Your co-worker thinks you can't do a task. You agree. (BTS 5)

a. はい、できます。 *Hai, dekimasu.*

b. いいえ、できません。 *Iie, dekimasen.*

c. はい、できません。 *Hai, dekimasen.*

11. You invite an office visitor to drink some tea. (BTS 11)

a. いただきますか。 *Itadakimasu ka.*

b. 飲^のみませんか。 *Nomimasen ka.*

c. ウーロン茶^{うろんちゃ}じゃないですか。 *Uuroncha ja nai desu ka.*

12. You ask your friend where the keys to the cabinet are. (BTS 28)

a. どうですか。 *Doo desu ka.*

b. どれですか。 *Dore desu ka.*

c. どっちですか。 *Dotchi desu ka.*

13. Hiragana is not used to write _____. (BTL 1)

    a. inflections
    b. Arabic numerals
    c. function words

14. Hiragana symbols have their origin in _____. (BTL 1)

    a. kanji characters
    b. spoken language
    c. technological advances

15. A dot between a series of symbols indicates _____. (BTL 2)

    a. the end of a quotation
    b. that they are separate words
    c. that something has been omitted

16. Two small dots or slashes "at the top right of a symbol indicate _____. (BTL 2)

    a. a direct quote
    b. the consonant value of the symbol changes from voiceless to voiced
    c. the consonant value of the symbol changes from voiced to voiceless

なん じ
何時ですか?

Nan-ji desu ka?

What time is it?

いそ まわ
急がば回れ   *Isogaba maware*
More haste, less speed.
(Literally, 'If you are in a hurry, go the long way.')

◆ **Scene 3-1 練習** *Renshuu* **Practice**

Answer sheet templates are provided in Appendix B for the Assessment sections.

理解実演練習 *Rikai jitsuen renshuu* **Comprehension and performance practice**

 3-1-1CP Asking about acronyms (BTS 1, 4, 5)

Ask Matsuura-san the meaning of an acronym, following the pattern in the example. Write down what you find out.

You	JLCって何ですか？	*JLC tte nan desu ka?*	What is JLC?
Matsuura-san	ジャパニーズ・ランゲージ・クラブのことですね。	*Japanese Language Club no koto desu ne.*	It means Japanese Language Club.

Ex. 1.   JLC   <u>Japanese Language Club</u>

Ex. 2.   JR   <u>Japan Rail</u>

3.   NG   _____

4.   OL   _____

5.   CM   _____

6.   JSO   _____

3-1-2P Agreeing with an opinion (BTS 2)

Agree with Kanda-san based on the illustration and the pattern in the example.

Ex. 1.

Kanda-san	きれいですねえ。	*Kiree desu nee.*	It's beautiful, isn't it.
You	そうですねえ。きれいなケーキですねえ。	*Soo desu nee. Kiree na keeki desu nee.*	It is. It's a beautiful cake, isn't it.

Ex. 2.

Kanda-san	難しいですねえ。	*Muzukashii desu nee.*	It's difficult, isn't it.
You	そうですねえ。難しい日本語ですねえ。	*Soo desu nee. Muzu-kashii nihongo desu nee.*	It is. It's difficult Japanese, isn't it.

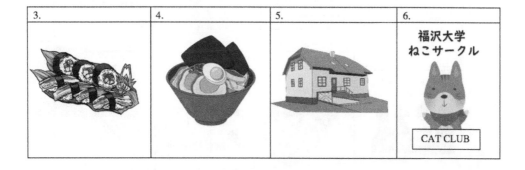

3-1-3P Confirming the topic before answering the question (BTS 2)

Listen to Yamada-san's question. Confirm the topic and then agree, following the pattern in the example.

Ex. 1.

| Yamada-san | 大きいですか？ | *Ookii desu ka?* | Is it big? |
| You | 神田さんの会社ですか？ そうですね。 | *Kanda-san no kaisha desu ka? Soo desu ne.* | Kanda-san's company? Yes, it is. |

Ex. 2.

| Yamada-san | 遠いですか？ | *Tooi desu ka?* | Is it far? |
| You | 寺田さんのお宅ですか？ そうですね。 | *Terada-san no otaku desu ka? Soo desu ne.* | Terada-san's home? Yes, it is. |

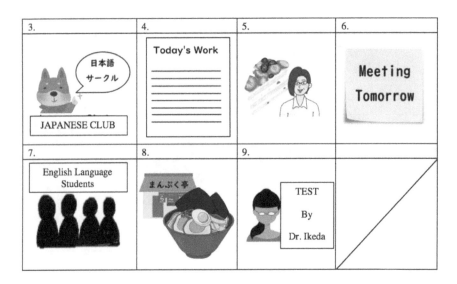

68

3-1-4P Picking up on a topic (BTS 4)

Pick up on a topic and ask Miyazaki-san a question about it, based on the information given. See how much of Miyazaki-san's response you can get. It may contain some unfamiliar expressions.

Ex. 1.

| You | 日本の大学って高いですか？ | *Nihon no daigaku tte takai desu ka?* | Are Japanese universities expensive? |
| Miyazaki-san | そうですねえ。高いですね。 | *Soo desu nee. Takai desu ne.* | Yes, I suppose they are expensive. |

Ex. 2.

| You | ロシア語って難しいですか？ | *Roshiago tte muzukashii desu ka?* | Is Russian difficult? |
| Miyazaki-san | すっごく難しいです！ | *Suggoku muzukashii desu!* | Yes, it's really difficult! |

3.	4.	5.
Is Waseda University in Tokyo?	Is University of Tokyo large?	Where did Miyazaki-san go to high school?

3-1 腕試し *Udedameshi* Tryout

1. Introduce yourself to a Japanese exchange student and find out his/her home university.
2. Introduce yourself to a Japanese professional and find out what company s/he works for.

♦ **Scene 3-2 練習 *Renshuu* Practice**

理解練習 *Rikai renshuu* Comprehension practice

 3-2-1C What's going on? (BTS 12)

Select the option that best corresponds to what the speaker thinks or does.

Ex. 1.	☒ It is Kanda-san	☐ It's not Kanda-san	☐ An invitation
Ex. 2.	☐ It is Kanda-san	☒ It's not Kanda-san	☐ An invitation
3.	☐ It is today	☐ It's not today	☐ An invitation
4.	☐ It is difficult	☐ It's not difficult	☐ An invitation
5.	☐ It is tomorrow	☐ It's not tomorrow	☐ An invitation
6.	☐ It is cheap	☐ It's not cheap	☐ An invitation
7.	☐ He can do it	☐ He can't do it	☐ An invitation
8.	☐ It is Shirai-san	☐ It's not Shirai-san	☐ An invitation
9.	☐ It is expensive	☐ It's not expensive	☐ An invitation
10.	☐ It is medicine	☐ It's not medicine	☐ An invitation
11.	☐ He understands	☐ He doesn't understand	☐ An invitation
12.	☐ He will begin	☐ He won't begin	☐ An invitation
13.	☐ He will do it	☐ He won't do it	☐ An invitation
14.	☐ It is pretty	☐ It's not pretty	☐ An invitation
15.	☐ It is far away	☐ It's not far away	☐ An invitation
16.	☐ He has it	☐ He doesn't have it	☐ An invitation
17.	☐ He will go	☐ He won't go	☐ An invitation
18.	☐ It is big	☐ It's not big	☐ An invitation
19.	☐ He will eat	☐ He won't eat	☐ An invitation

3-2-2P Saying "let's do it!" (BTS 8)

When Matsumoto-san asks if the two of you will do something, respond affirmatively with enthusiasm.

Ex. 1.	Matsumoto-san	行きますか?	*Ikimasu ka?*	Are we going to go?
	You	はい、行きましょう。	*Hai, ikimashoo.*	Yes, let's go.
Ex. 2.	Matsumoto-san	待ちますか?	*Machimasu ka?*	Are we going to wait?
	You	はい、待ちましょう。	*Hai, Machimashoo.*	Yes, let's wait.

3-2-3P Confirming the time of an event (BTS 9, 12)

When Yamada-san checks on the time of an event, respond based on the list of events and times below.

Ex. 1.	Yamada-san	日本語の授業って、10時半ですね。	*Nihongo no jugyoo tte, juu-jihan desu ne.*	The Japanese class is at 10:30, right?
	You	ええ、１０時半ですね。	*Ee, juu-ji han desu ne.*	Yes, it's at 10:30.
Ex. 2.	Yamada-san	明日の会議って、３時ですね。	*Ashita no kaigi tte, san-ji desu ne.*	Tomorrow's meeting is at 3:00, right?
	You	あのう、２時じゃないですか。	*Anoo, ni-ji ja nai desu ka.*	Uhm, isn't it at 2:00?

English class	9:30
Japanese class	10:30
Tanaka-san's arrival	12:30
Dr. Yamamoto's arrival	13:00
Today's meeting	16:00
Tomorrow's meeting	14:00

3-2-4P Telling who isn't coming (BTS 7, 10)

At a meeting the group's leader notices that someone is missing. Tell her either that person is absent today, or that person and Tanaka-san are absent today, based on the illustration.

Ex. 1.

Leader	ええっと、ジェームス君は？	*Eetto, Jeemusu-kun wa?*	Uhm, what about James-kun?
You	あ、ジェームス君、今日はお休みです。	*A, Jeemusu-kun, kyoo wa oyasumi desu.*	Oh, James-kun—he is absent today.

Ex. 2.

Leader	じゃあ、始めましょう。あ、坂本先生は？	*Jaa, hajimemashoo. A, Sakamoto-sensee wa?*	Okay, let's start. Oh, what about Sakamoto-sensei?
You	あ、坂本先生と田中さん、今日はお休みです。	*A, Sakamoto-sensee to Tanaka-san, kyoo wa oyasumi desu.*	Oh, Sakamoto-sensei and Tanaka-san—they are off today.

7.	8.	9.	
TANAKA		TANAKA	

3-2 腕試し *Udedameshi* Tryout

1. Confirm the time of an event with a friend or acquaintance.
2. Confirm who will attend a certain event.
3. Ask a friend or acquaintance if s/he understands any of the languages that you speak.

◆ Scene 3-3 練習 *Renshuu* Practice

理解練習 *Rikai renshuu* Comprehension practice

 ### 3-3-1C What's right? (BTS 13, 14)

Listen to two people talk through a slight difference of opinion. Write down what they finally agree on.

Ex. 1. It's Spanish._____

Ex. 2. Professor Sakamoto's homework isn't difficult.

3. _____

4. _____

5. _____

6. _____

7. _____

8. _____

 ### 3-3-2C What's the loanword? (BTS 14)

In each conversation you will hear an English loanword. Identify the original English word, and write it down in the space provided. The type of item under discussion is provided.

Ex. 1. Name: Peter_____

Ex. 2. Destination: Europe_____

3. Food: _____

4. Sport: _____

5. City: _____

6. Music: _____

7. Beverage: _____

実演練習 *Jitsuen renshuu* Performance practice

3-3-3P Making explicit corrections (BTS 13)

When Mizuno-san, your senior colleague, brings up a topic, correct her based on the illustration. Maintain the appropriate level of formality.

Ex. 1.

**Meeting
10:30**

Mizuno-san	今日の１０時の会議、英語ですよ。	*Kyoo no 10-ji no kaigi, Eego desu yo.*	Today's 10:00 meeting is in English!
You	そうですか。あ、会議、１０時じゃなくて１０時半ですけど……。	*Soo desu ka. A, kaigi, 10-ji ja nakute 10-ji-han desu kedo . . .*	I see. Oh, the meeting is not at 10:00; it's at 10:30. . . .

Ex. 2.

Mizuno-san	このジャンさんの傘、きれいですね。	*Kono Jan-san no kasa, kiree desu ne.*	(This) Zhang-san's umbrella is pretty, isn't it.
You	そうですね。あ、それ、ジャンさんじゃなくて、ジェームスさんの傘ですけど……。	*Soo desu ne. A, sore, Jan-san ja nakute Jeemusu-san no kasa desu kedo . . .*	Yes, oh, that isn't Zhang-san's; it's James-san's umbrella . . .

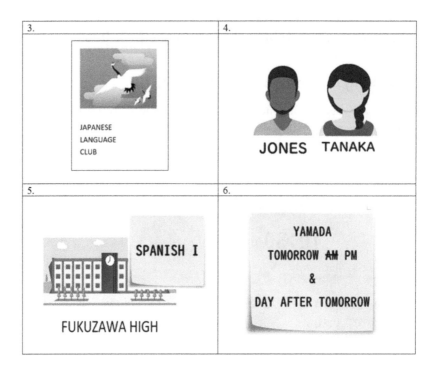

🎧 3-3-4P Making corrections on mistaken identities (BTS 13)

When Tanaka-san, who is a junior member of your group, inquires about a new member, make a correction based on the information on the list below.

Ex. 1.	Tanaka-san	張さんって韓国人ですか？	*Choo-san tte, kankokujin desu ka?*	Is Cho-san Korean?
	You	いや、韓国人じゃなくて、中国人です。	*Iya, kankokujin ja nakute, chuugokujin desu.*	No, she is Chinese, not Korean.
Ex. 2.	Tanaka-san	ジェームス君ってアメリカ人ですか？	*Jeemusu-kun tte, amerikajin desu ka?*	Is James-kun American?
	You	いや、アメリカ人じゃなくて、フランス人です。	*Iya, amerikajin ja nakute, furansujin desu.*	No, he is French, not American.

Name	Age	From
Amy Zhang	20	China
James Napoleon	19	France
Kei Mizuno	32	USA (person of Japanese heritage)
May Kadono	16	Unknown (but not Japan)
Jay Rodriguez	23	USA
Natalie Baron	26	Russia

3-3 腕試し *Udedameshi* Tryout

When you find an appropriate opportunity, make one focused and explicit correction on a question or statement that your Japanese friend makes (in Japanese!). An appropriate opportunity means that your relative relationship with that person, and the situation, allows you to make such a correction. Use this strategy with care!

◆ **Scene 3-4 練習 *Renshuu* Practice**

理解練習 *Rikai renshuu* Comprehension practice

3-4-1C What time is the train? (BTS 19)

Ishikawa-san is coming to visit, and you are planning to meet at the train station. Listen to his arrival time and write it down so that you don't forget. Use a.m. and p.m. as appropriate.

Ex. 1.   3:47 p.m. _____

Ex. 2.   6:21 p.m. _____

   3. _____

   4. _____

   5. _____

   6. _____

   7. _____

   8. _____

   9. _____

3-4-2C Where did they study that language? (BTS 15)

A man is asking his new work associate about her foreign language study. Identify the language and where the woman studied it. If you hear something unfamiliar, answer using the information you are able to identify.

Ex. 1.   Korean   Peking University

Ex. 2.   Japanese   A university in Ohio (The Ohio State University)

   3. _____   _____

   4. _____   _____

   5. _____   _____

   6. _____   _____

   7. _____   _____

   8. _____   _____

実演練習 *Jitsuen renshuu* Performance practice

3-4-3P Confirming that you've heard it right (BTS 16, 19, 20, 21)

In the office, Kawada-san, your work associate, asks you to meet her at a particular time and place. Repeat back the time and place to confirm that you've got the right information. She may use a few unfamiliar expressions. Focus on the key information.

Ex. 1.	Kawada-san	じゃあ、あさって午前１１時に現地で。	*Jaa, asatte gozen juuichi-ji ni genchi de.*	Then, the day after tomorrow at 11:00 a.m. at the place.
	You	あさって午前１１時に現地ですね?わかりました。	*Asatte gozen juuichi-ji ni genchi desu ne? Wakarimashita.*	That's the day after tomorrow at 11:00 a.m. at the place, right? Got it.
Ex. 2.	Kawada-san	ええと、今度の会議は午後１時に、大垣商会でいたしますから、よろしくお願いします。	*Eeto, kondo no kaigi wa gogo ichi-ji ni Oogaki-shookai de itashi-masu kara, yoroshiku onegai-shimasu.*	Uhm, the next meeting will be at 1:00 p.m. at Ogaki-shokai, so please be prepared.
	You	午後１時に、大垣商会ですね?わかりました。	*Gogo ichi-ji ni Ooga-ki-shookai desu ne? Wakarimashita.*	That's at 1:00 p.m. at Ogaki-shokai, right? Got it.

3-4 腕試し *Udedameshi* Tryout

1. Try making an appointment to meet, to talk, to eat together, etc., for a specified time in the future.
2. When someone tells you information that you need to act on, such as the date or time of an event you will attend, confirm the information by repeating it back to the person.

◆ **Scene 3-5 練習 *Renshuu* Practice**

理解練習 *Rikai renshuu* Comprehension practice

 3-5-1C Getting the details

Paul, a study abroad student from the US, has two conversations with two different people, both curious about his experiences and plans. For each conversation, listen for some particular details and write down what you find out.

Conversation I

Ex. 1.	Where Paul studied Japanese	At graduate school _____
Ex. 2.	Paul's homestay family	The Mizunos _____
3.	A great feature of the homestay	_____
4.	Distance from school	_____
5.	Test date(s)	_____
6.	Test subject(s)	_____

Conversation II

7.	Their choice of food for lunch	_____
8.	Location of the eatery	_____
9.	Potential drawback of the location	_____
10.	The correction Paul receives	_____

 3-5-2C How many are there? (BTS 25, 26)

Sasha and Kanda-san are checking the inventory of office supplies. Circle the item they appear to be talking about, and write down how many there are.

Ex. 1.	170 _____	notebooks	paper	(pens)
Ex. 2.	200 _____	notebooks	(paper)	pencils
3.	_____	notebooks	paper	mechanical pencils
4.	_____	notebooks	paper	pens

5.	_____	notebooks	paper	pens
6.	_____	notebooks	paper	mechanical pencils
7.	_____	notebooks	paper	pencils
8.	_____	notebooks	paper	pens

実演練習 *Jitsuen renshuu* Performance practice

3-5-3P Stating unit prices (BTS 22, 25, 26, 27)

You and your colleague Terada-san are going over some items for potential purchase. As Terada-san asks about an item, say the price of that item in the catalogue.

Ex. 1.	Terada-san	ノートは？	*Nooto wa?*	What about notebooks?
	You	このノート、どうですか？１冊２００円ですけど‥‥‥。	*Kono nooto, doo desu ka? Is-satsu 200-en desu kedo . . .*	How about these notebooks? They are 200-yen each . . .
Ex. 2.	Terada-san	小さい傘は？	*Chiisai kasa wa?*	What about small umbrellas?
	You	この小さい傘、どうですか？　一本８００円ですけど‥‥‥。	*Kono chiisai kasa, doo desu ka? Ip-pon 800-en desu kedo . . .*	How about these small umbrellas? They are 800 yen each . . .

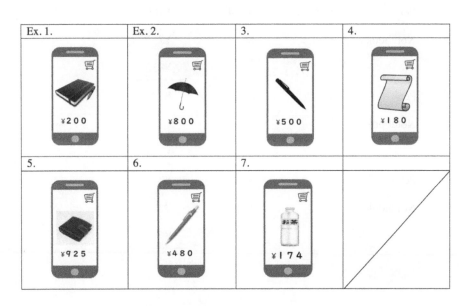

81

3-5-4P Doing some quick math (BTS 25, 26, 27)

You are helping your friend Yuya-kun plan some purchases. Write down the prices and quantities he mentions and provide the total.

Ex. 1.	Yuya-kun	1本10円のペン8本と1冊120円のノート6冊ですね。	*Ip-pon juu-en no pen, hap-pon to, is-satsu hyakunijuu-en no nooto roku-satsu desu ne.*	It's 8 pens at 10-yen each and 6 notebooks at 120-yen each.
	You	じゃあ、全部で800円ですね。	*Jaa, zenbu de happyaku-en desu ne.*	Then that's 800-yen, total, right?
Ex. 2.	Yuya-kun	1本25円のペン4本と1冊250円のノート3冊ですね。	*Ip-pon nijuugo-en no pen, yon-hon to, is-satsu nihyakugojuu-en no nooto san-satsu desu ne.*	It's 4 pens at 25-yen each and 3 notebooks at 250-yen each.
	You	じゃあ、全部で850円ですね。	*Jaa, zenbu de happyakugojuu-en desu ne.*	Then that's 850-yen, total, right?

Use the worksheet below

	Items	Unit Price	Quantity		TOTAL
Ex. 1.	Pens	¥10	X	8	¥80
	Notebooks	¥120	X	6	¥720
					¥800
Ex. 2.	Pens	¥25	X	4	¥100
	Notebooks	¥250	X	3	¥750
					¥850
3.	Pens	¥	X		¥
	Notebooks	¥	X		¥
					¥
4.	Pens	¥	X		¥
	Notebooks	¥	X		¥
					¥

5.	Pens	¥	X	¥
	Notebooks	¥	X	¥
				¥
6.	Pens	¥	X	¥
	Notebooks	¥	X	¥
				¥

3-5 腕試し *Udedameshi* Tryout

Ask a Japanese friend or acquaintance if s/he thinks the price of a certain item is expensive or not.

◆ Scene 3-6 練習 *Renshuu* Practice

理解練習 *Rikai renshuu* Comprehension practice

3-6-1C Identifying owners (BTS 29, 30)

Listen to the conversations in which various people identify the owners of certain items and match the illustrations of the items with the faces of their owners. Draw a line between the item and its presumed owner.

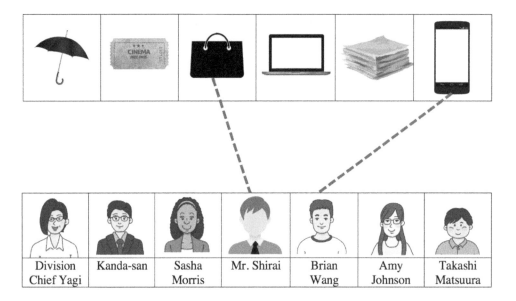

実演練習 *Jitsuen renshuu* Performance practice

3-6-2P Claiming ownership (BTS 29)

Your office mate Eriko is cleaning the office. As she picks up various items, claim your ownership, lest she throw them away!

| Ex. 1. | Eriko | これは？ | *Kore wa?* | What about this one? |

| | You | あ、私 (or 僕) のです。私 (or 僕) の傘。すみません。 | *A, watashi (or boku) no desu. Watashi (or boku) no kasa. Sumimasen.* | Oh, that's mine. That's my umbrella. Sorry. |

| Ex. 2. | Eriko | これは？ | *Kore wa?* | What about this one? |

| | You | あ、私 (or 僕) のです。私 (or 僕) のカバン。すみません。 | *A, watashi (or boku) no desu. Watashi (or boku) no kaban. Sumimasen.* | Oh, that's mine. That's my bag. Sorry. |

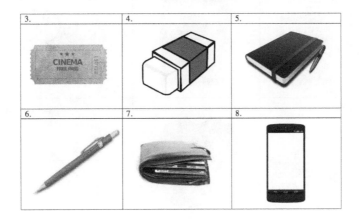

 ### 3-6-3P Locating items (BTS 29, 30)

You can't find something you normally carry with you, so you called the office to ask Shoji-san, a new intern, if he can find the item there. Use the illustration as the guide for the missing item in each conversation.

Ex. 1.	Shoji-san	はい、庄司です。	*Hai, Shooji desu.*	Hello, this is Shoji.
		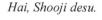		
	You	あ、すみません。あの、私のスマホ、そっちにありますか?	*A, sumimasen. Ano, watashi no sumaho, sotchi ni arimasu ka?*	Uh, sorry, um, is my smartphone there?
Ex. 2.	Shoji-san	はい、庄司です。	*Hai, Shooji desu.*	Hello, this is Shoji.
		Blue		
	You	あ、すみません。あの、私の青いカバン、そっちにありますか?	*A, sumimasen. Ano, watashi no aoi kaban, sotchi ni arimasu ka?*	Uh, sorry, um, is my blue bag there?

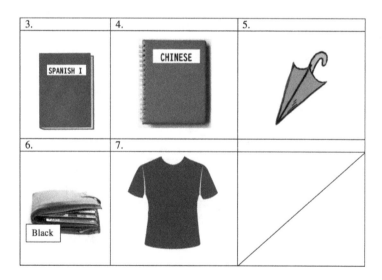

3-6 腕試し *Udedameshi* Tryout

Think of a city in Japan where you don't know if a university exists or not. Find out from a Japanese friend or colleague if there is a university in that city.

読み練習 *Yomi-renshuu* Reading practice

3-7-1R Asking questions

Read the following questions and indicate whether each is a yes/no question or a wh-question.

Ex. 1.	この会議、何時ですか。	Yes/no	(Wh)
Ex. 2.	あの学生、東大ですか。	(Yes/no)	Wh
3.	たかし君、高校生ですか。	Yes/no	Wh
4.	あちらの先生、どなたですか。	Yes/no	Wh
5.	その傘、神田さんのですか。	Yes/no	Wh
6.	赤坂さんの傘、どれですか。	Yes/no	Wh
7.	須田さんの傘、どこですか。	Yes/no	Wh
8.	あの先生、どちらの大学ですか。	Yes/no	Wh

3-7-2R Inviting someone to do something together

Match the following topics to appropriate invitations. While some of the invitations might suit multiple topics, you may use each option only once.

Ex. 1.	レポート、みんなで	_f_	a. 見ませんか
Ex. 2.	会議、またあした	_b_	b. しませんか
3.	おいしそうですね。	___	c. 帰りませんか
4.	6時に	___	d. 飲みませんか
5.	現地で	___	e. 会いませんか
6.	サッカーのゲーム	___	f. 書きませんか

文字練習 *Moji renshuu* Symbol practice

Use the Symbol Practice sheets in Appendix A to practice *hiragana* characters #25–28 for Scene 3-7.

3-7-3W Nouns modifying nouns

What kind of nouns are they? Write の if they describe other nouns with the Particle の. Write な if they describe other nouns with the Particle な.

Ex. 1. 日本語<u>　の　</u>本

Ex. 2. 大丈夫<u>　な　</u>水

   3. だめ＿＿＿スマホ

   4. 4時＿＿＿会議

   5. 面白そう＿＿＿友達

   6. 先生＿＿＿傘

   7. スマホ＿＿＿アプリ

   8. 5ドル＿＿＿ノートときれい＿＿＿消しゴム

読み練習 *Yomi-renshuu* Reading practice

3-8-1R Giving someone new information

Provide your personal opinions with regards to the following topics.

Ex. 1. 神田さんですか？　（おもしろい・おもしろくない）ですよ。

Ex. 2. 私のスマホの会社ですか？　（いい・よくない）ですよ。

3. そばですか？　（好き・好きじゃない）ですよ。

4. ルームメートですか？　（います・いません）よ。

5. 私の学校ですか？　（大学・大学じゃない）ですよ。

6. 日本語のクラスですか？　（難しい・難しくない）ですよ。

7. 今日ですか？　（忙しい・忙しくない）ですよ。

8. 今日の宿題ですか？　（あります・ありません）よ。

3-8-2R X or Y?

What are they talking about? Select the topic for each of the following questions. You may only use each option once.

a. 会議　　b. 英語　c. 須田さん　d. コーヒー　e. アニメ　f. テニス　g. 6時

Ex. 1. ___f___ はしますか、しないですか。

Ex. 2. ___e___ は見ますか、見ないですか。

3. _____ はありますか、ないですか。

4. _____ はできますか、できないですか。

5. _____ に帰りますか、帰らないですか。

6. _____ は飲みますか、飲まないですか。

7. _____ は行きますか、行かないですか。

文字練習 *Moji renshuu* Symbol practice

Use the Symbol Practice sheets in Appendix A to practice *hiragana* characters #29-32 for Scene 3-8.

3-8-3W Filling in the blanks

Fill in the blanks with either は or も or け(れ)ど.

Ex. 1. 学生＿＿は＿＿いくらですか。

Ex. 2. あしたの会議です＿＿けれど＿＿何時ですか。

3. あの傘です＿＿＿＿＿＿、だれのですか。

4. これ、部長のですか?あれ＿＿＿＿＿＿ですか。

5. あしたの会議です＿＿＿＿＿＿、行きますか。

6. 坂本さん＿＿＿＿＿＿、どちらの大学ですか。

7. 今日＿＿＿＿＿＿明日＿＿＿＿＿＿お休みですか。

8. あの東大の先生です＿＿＿＿＿＿、英語の先生ですか。

読み練習 *Yomi-renshuu* Reading practice

3-9-1R Let's do X together.

Select what is omitted in each of the consultations below. You may use each option only once.

a. お茶　b. 会議　c. これ　d. 何時ごろ　e. ちょっと　f. みんな　g. この

Ex. 1. ＿＿e＿＿ 休みましょうか。

Ex. 2. この＿＿a＿＿、飲みましょうか。

3. 今日、＿＿＿＿＿＿しましょうか。

4. ＿＿＿＿＿＿宿題、しましょうか。

5. 今日は＿＿＿＿＿＿帰りましょうか。

6. ＿＿＿＿＿＿は、大学で書きましょうか。

7. 何時ごろまた＿＿＿＿＿＿で会いましょうか。

3-9-2R Correcting information

Choose from the selections the correct information for each of the statements that follow.

a. 午後　b. ここ　c. あちら　d. 7時　e. あさって　f. 先生の　g. 傘　h. あれ

Ex. 1. 時時じゃなくて、＿＿d＿＿です。

Ex. 2. これじゃないですよ。＿＿h＿＿です。

3. こちらじゃなくて、＿＿＿＿＿＿ですよ。

4. 午前6時じゃなくて、＿＿＿＿＿＿6時です。

5. その授業、＿＿＿＿＿＿じゃありませんよ。

6. それ、白井先生の＿＿＿＿＿＿じゃないですよ。

7. あの会議はあしたじゃありませんよ。＿＿＿＿＿＿ですよ。

8. そのかばんは須田さんのですよ。＿＿＿＿＿＿じゃないですよ。

3-9-3R Uses of では de wa

Determine whether the following uses of では are used to make a transition or a negation.

Ex. 1.	では、また。	(Transition)	Negation
Ex. 2.	1冊ではありません。	Transition	(Negation)
3.	では、始めましょう。	Transition	Negation
4.	それでは、失礼します。	Transition	Negation
5.	今日ではありません。明日です。	Transition	Negation
6.	こちらではないです。あちらです。	Transition	Negation

書き練習 *Kaki-renshuu* Writing practice

文字練習 *Moji renshuu* Symbol practice

Use the Symbol Practice sheets in Appendix A to practice *hiragana* characters #33–45 for Scene 3-9.

 3-9-4W Using furigana

Listen to the voice message and write furigana for the name of each participant in a speech contest.

スピーチコンテスト出場者リスト

Ex. 1.　けん　たなか
　　　　ケン・田中

Ex. 2.　すざんぬ　つちや
　　　　スザンヌ・土屋

3.
　　　堀田　隆太

4.
　　　向井　芽衣

5.
　　　中井　良輔

6.
　　　ニクソン・古川

7.
　　　和田　由紀子

8.
　　　ヘンリー・平田

3-9-5W Using furigana

The following sets of name cards have some errors in their furigana. Compare the romanized scripts with the furigana and provide corrections as needed. Place a check mark (✓) if the furigana is right.

Ex. 1. Mr. Himesawa	Ex. 2. Ms. Furuta	3. Mr. Nunokawa	4. Ms. Homura
✔ ひめさわ 姫沢	る ふるた 古田	ねのかわ 布川	まむら 穂村
5. Ms. Beppu	6. Ms. Ryugasaki	7. Ms. Keyaki	8. Mr. Meguro
べっぷ 別府	りゅうがちき 龍ヶ崎	けやき 欅	ぬぐる 目黒

◆ 評価 *Hyooka* Assessment

Answer sheet templates are provided in Appendix B for the Assessment sections.

聞いてみよう *Kiite miyoo* Listening comprehension

Read the context, listen to the audio, and then answer the questions. If you hear something unfamiliar, rely on what you know to choose the correct answer.

1. Yagi-bucho is leading a division meeting.

    a. What does she check?
    b. What time was the meeting supposed to start?

2. Kanda-san just called Sasha on her office cell phone.

    a. What is Kanda-san looking for? What color is it?
    b. What feature does Sasha use to confirm that she has the right item?
    c. Who ultimately finds the item?

3. Kanda-san enters a small meeting room where a visitor has been waiting.

    a. What is the visitor's name?
    b. Where does the visitor work?
    c. Who else was Kanda-san expecting?
    d. What does he learn about that person?

4. Amy is attending a small gathering that Takashi is having at his dorm.

    a. Who are the students?
    b. Who is Sam?

5. Sasha is talking to another intern about something she sees on a website.

    a. What does Sasha initially check on?
    b. What does she ask the intern to do for her?
    c. How helpful is the intern?

6. After a Japanese Conversation Club meeting, Amy asks Takashi a question.

    a. What is Amy's initial question?
    b. Why does Amy ask this question?
    c. What does Takashi decide to do in the end?

7. Amy finds something that was left in the room after a meeting.

    a. What is the item that was left in the room?
    b. Who does Amy initially think it belongs to?
    c. What does the new word that Amy learns mean?

使ってみよう *Tsukatte miyoo* Dry run

Listen to the audio and respond according to the context.

1. (a) It's about 11:00 a.m. now. (b) The meeting is at 3:30 p.m. (c) Testing will be tomorrow at 10:00 a.m.
2. You have a Japanese friend who is eager to learn English. He has asked you to correct his English pronunciation carefully. He will pick up 5 items on your desk and say what they are in English. Correct his pronunciation as best as you can.
3. Your work associate is considering a purchase. When he tells you the price of the one that he is looking at, comment whether you think it's expensive or not expensive. Here are the common price ranges for the items that your associate will be talking about. (a) about $20; (b) $100–$150; (c) ¢60–¢80; (d) $500–$600; (e) $70–$80
4. You and your work associate are meeting a client at her office, but you are unsure of the location.
5. (a) Tanaka-san and Nakamura-san are scheduled for tomorrow. (b) Trains to Kyoto depart at 3:54 and 6:17. (c) Tanaka-san is scheduled for tomorrow and the day after tomorrow.

Now it's your turn to start the conversation based on the given context. Listen to how the other person reacts to you. For some items, you may not get a verbal response. If you hear something unfamiliar, rely on what you know to choose the correct answer.

6. You are taking a Japanese visitor out for some ice cream. He knows some English but is more comfortable in Japanese. Find out a good Japanese equivalent of the following expressions: (a) ice cream sundae; (b) credit card; (c) takeout; (d) trash; (e) sweet; (f) too much.
7. You see a blue bag that you think belongs to your friend Ms. Zhang. Check with a senior person.
8. Your supervisor is showing you a short proposal that another person prepared. You notice an error. First, (a) suggest where the error is. Then, (b) suggest that the number of rods involved is not 690, but 890.
9. Your senior team member just told you who will be joining you at an upcoming event, but you are not sure if he said Shimizu or Shimazu. Indicate that there was a little glitch in your listening and find out which it is.
10. You are talking with your senior team member about an upcoming event. Find out where it will be held.
11. You have just learned that you are to come to the library at 2:00 p.m. Confirm the time and place succinctly.
12. A senior student is wondering where to wait for a group of visitors. Suggest that you wait at the university.
13. You heard that Fukuzawa University sends students to study abroad at Clinton University, but you're not sure where that is. Ask Sakata-san, who works in Fukuzawa University's study abroad office, where Clinton University is.

Act 3

何時ですか?

読んでみよう *Yonde miyoo* Contextualized reading

1. Here is a handwritten note on a container found on a table in an office:

これ、よかったられはさんでどうぞ.
M. I.

   a. What does the writer want the reader to do?

The following examples assume you are reading the texts with some help from a furigana-generating website, browser add-on, app, etc.

2. An email from your coworker, Yamamoto-san, with an attachment:

Subject: 携帯

これ、白井さんのじゃありませんか。

山本

---

   a. What is Yamamoto-san checking on?

3. An email from a coworker, Terada-san:

Subject：Re: 会議の時間

すみません、あしたの会議の時間ですけど、4時じゃなくて4時半じゃありませんか。

寺田

---

   a. What is the topic of the email?
   b. What correction does Terada-san provide?

4. A text message from your classmate at college:

DOKOKA   12:15
Amy Johnson

今日_{きょう}の宿題_{しゅくだい}、みんなで大学_{だいがく}の
図書館_{としょかん}でしませんか。

   a. What is your classmate suggesting? Provide details.

 ## 書き取り *Kakitori* Dictation

Listen, imagine the context, repeat silently what you hear, then write it down.

1. _____。
2. _____。
3. _____。
4. _____。
5. _____。
6. _____。
7. _____。
8. _____。
9. _____。
10. _____。
11. _____。
12. _____。
13. _____。

書いてみよう *Kaite miyoo* Contextualized writing

Consider the context provided and write a note according to the directions.

1. You have found a folder left in the conference room. On a sticky note attached to the folder, write a memo asking whose it is.

2. You are returning a plastic container to your neighbor who gave you a piece of pie. You've made some cookies in return and placed them in the container. On a sticky note attached to the container, write a thank-you note and invite your neighbors (everyone in the household) to have these (cookies) if they would like to . . .

3. You are recommending a game to your colleague. On a sticky note attached to the game, write a note, indicating that it is, as expected, very interesting. Invite your colleague to play it on the day after tomorrow.

4. Provide corrections for the following name cards for Sato Takeru (Satou Takeru) and Nunokawa Ryutaro (Nunokawa Ryuutarou).

知ってる? *Shitte'ru?* What do you know?

Select the most appropriate option and write the letter in the space on your answer sheet.

1. You've been asked about a computer. You respond:
   新しい先生＿＿＿＿パソコンですよ。 *Atarashii sensee _____ pasokon desu yo.* (BTS 2)
   a. な *na*
   b. の *no*
   c. に *ni*

2. You're enthusiastic about a new club at school.
   好き＿＿＿スポーツは? *Suki ____supootsu wa?* (BTS 2)
   a. な *na*
   b. の *no*
   c. に *ni*

3. You're wondering about the time of the class.
何時____授業ですか。 *Nan-ji _____jugyoo desu ka.* (BTS 2, 20)

    a. な *na*
    b. の *no*
    c. で *de*

4. You're curious about the meaning of "KC".
KC____カンザスシティのことですね? *KC ____ kanzasu shiti no koto desu ne?*
(BTS 4, 5, 14)

    a. に *ni*
    b. で *de*
    c. って *tte*

5. You're wondering what the Japanese word is for something.
日本語で_____といいますか。 *Nihongo de _____to iimasu ka.* (BTS 3)

    a. 何 *nani*
    b. どう *doo*
    c. 何 *nan*

6. You explain the meaning of *amefuto.*
アメリカンフットボール_____。 *Amerikan futtobooru _____.* (BTS 4, 5)

    a って言います *tte iimasu*
    b. のことです *no koto desu*
    c. とのことです *to no koto desu*

7. You suggest that you and your co-worker go home together.
一緒に_____。 *Issho ni_____.* (BTS 8)

    a. 帰りません *kaerimasen*
    b. 帰ります *kaerimasu*
    c. 帰りましょう *kaerimashoo*

8. You've been discussing sports.
サッカー____テニス____しますよ。 *Sakkaa ____tenisu____ shimasu yo.* (BTS 31)

    a. も *mo* も *mo*
    b. と *to* と *to*
    c. も *mo* と *to*

9. You've been asked if you eat both sushi and sashimi. You reply:
寿司____食べますが。 *Sushi ____ tabemasu ga.* (BTS 7, 10, 15)

    a. は *wa*
    b. と *to*
    c. で *de*

10. You ask your coworker about an upcoming meeting.

あの会議____ 3時半じゃないですか。 *Ano kaigi_____san-ji-han ja nai desu ka.*
(BTS 7, 10, 20)

    a. に *ni*

    b. は *wa*

    c. と *to*

11. You've been asked where the meeting will be held. You reply:

図書館____あります。 *Toshokan ____arimasu.* (BTS 15, 30)

    a. で *de*

    b. と *to*

    c. に *ni*

12. You've been asked where the tickets are.

あちら____あります。 *Achira ____ arimasu.* (BTS 15, 30)

    a. に *ni*

    b. で *de*

    c. は *wa*

13. You finally realized that the destination is, after all, quite far away.

_____遠いですねえ。_____*tooi desu nee.* (BTS 6, 11)

    a. なるほど *Naruhodo*

    b. やっぱり *Yappari*

    c. ちょっと *Chotto*

14. You suggest that you meet in the lobby.

ロビー_____会いましょうか。 *Robii _____ aimashoo ka.* (BTS 7, 15, 30)

    a. で *de*

    b. に *ni*

    c. は *wa*

15. You correct Ms. Yamada's mistaken assumption.

それ、日本語_____中国語ですよ。 *Sore, nihongo _____chuugokugo desu yo.*
(BTS 13c)

    a. じゃない *ja nai*

    b. じゃなくて *ja nakute*

    c. じゃないです *ja nai desu*

16. All Japanese loanwords_____. (BTS 14)

    a. mean the same as the original word

    b. undergo a pronunciation change

c. are imported from English

17. You've been asked how many books you will buy. You respond:
三_{さん}_____買_かいます。 *San-_____ kaimasu.* (BTS 26)
a. 冊_{さつ} *satsu*
b. 本_{ぼん} *bon*
c. 個_こ *ko*

18. You ask about how many tickets they have.
何_{なん}____ありますか。 *Nan-_____arimasu ka.* (BTS 26)
a. 個_こ *ko*
b. 枚_{まい} *mai*
c. 冊_{さつ} *satsu*

19. You tell your new acquaintance how long you intend to wait in the lobby.
１０分_{ぶん}_____待_まちます。 *Jup-pun _____ machimasu.* (BTS 19)
a. に *ni*
b. ごろ *goro*
c. Ø

20. You're wondering about the whereabouts of Kanda-san.
大学_{だいがく}_____いますか。 *Daigaku ____ imasu ka.* (BTS 30)
a. へ *e*
b. は *wa*
c. に *ni*

21. You've been asked if the laptop is yours. You reply:
私_{わたし}_____じゃないです。 *Watashi ____ ja nai desu.* (BTS 2, 29)
a. の *no*
b. な *na*
c. Ø

22. Completion (classifiers) (BTS 26)
四_{よん}_____ *Yon-_____*
a. 分_{ぶん} *pun*
b. 時_じ *ji*
c. 円_{えん} *en*

23. 九_{きゅう}_____ *Kyuu-____* (BTS 26)
a. 枚_{まい} *mai*

Act 3
何時ですか?

b. 時 *ji*

c. 分 *pun*

24. 十_____ *Juu-_____* (BTS 26)

    a. 分 *pun*

    b. 円 *en*

    c. セント *sento*

25. 八_____ *Hachi-_____* (BTS 26)

    a. 冊 *satsu*

    b. 枚 *mai*

    c. 本 *hon*

26. You want to know if the small one also costs 100 yen.

    小さい_____も１００円ですか。*Chiisai ____ mo 100-en desu ka.* (BTS 28)

    a. な *na*

    b. に *ni*

    c. の *no*

27. Long consonants (*soku-on)* are represented in horizontal writing in hiragana by _____. (BTL 2)

    a. a small つ slightly lower than other symbols

    b. writing the hiragana symbol twice

    c. writing the hiragana symbol lower than other symbols

28. *Yoo-on* refers to _____. (BTL 3)

    a. the vowel sounds in や, ゆ, and よ

    b. two long vowels

    c. the や in じゃ

29. Japanese fonts _____. (BTL 5)

    a. are limited stylistically

    b. vary a good deal

    c. are used for the alphabet

れんらく き
連絡来ました?

Renraku kimashita?

Did they get in touch?

とき　かね
時は金なり *Toki wa kane nari*

Time is money.

◆ **Scene 4-1 練習 *Renshuu* Practice**

理解練習 *Rikai renshuu* Comprehension practice

4-1-1C Non-past or past? (BTS 1)

Listen to each statement, and mark each as "past" or "non-past."

Ex. 1. ☒ Past ☐ Non-past
Ex. 2. ☐ Past ☒ Non-past
3. ☐ Past ☐ Non-past
4. ☐ Past ☐ Non-past
5. ☐ Past ☐ Non-past
6. ☐ Past ☐ Non-past
7. ☐ Past ☐ Non-past
8. ☐ Past ☐ Non-past
9. ☐ Past ☐ Non-past
10. ☐ Past ☐ Non-past
11. ☐ Past ☐ Non-past
12. ☐ Past ☐ Non-past

実演練習 *Jitsuen renshuu* Performance practice

4-1-2P It wasn't like that. (BTS 1)

Yoshida-san, a colleague slightly older than you, asks about your recent experience. Tell her that things weren't as she suggests.

Ex. 1.

¥2679

Yoshida-san	高かったですか？	*Takakatta desu ka?*	Was it expensive?
You	いえ、高くなかったですよ。	*Ie, takakunakatta desu yo.*	No, it wasn't expensive.

Ex. 2.

Yoshida-san	きれいでしたか？	*Kiree deshita ka?*	Was it clean?
You	いえ、きれいじゃなかったですよ。	*Ie, kiree ja nakatta desu yo.*	No, it wasn't clean.

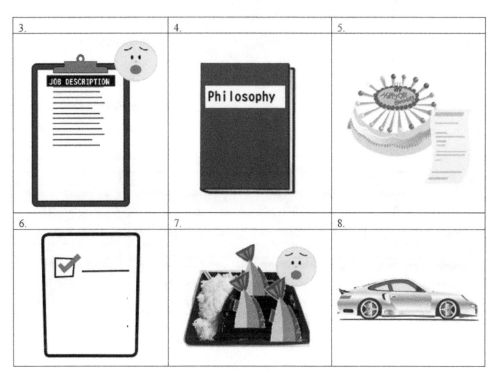

4-1-3P Refuting an idea (BTS 1)

Assure Nakamura-san, a club member who is a year older, that his negative assumptions are incorrect.

Ex. 1.

| Nakamura-san | 行かなかったですか？ | *Ikanakatta desu ka?* | Did they not go? |
| You | いえいえ、行きましたよ。 | *Ieie, ikimashita yo.* | No, they went. |

Ex. 2.

| Nakamura-san | 面白そうじゃなかったで すか？ | *Omoshirosoo ja nakatta desu ka?* | Did it not seem interesting? |
| You | いえいえ、面白そうでし たよ。 | *Ieie, omoshirosoo deshita yo.* | No, it seemed interesting. |

 ## 4-1-4P It costs about this much. (BTS 4)

Respond to Murata-san, a senior colleague, with approximate prices based on the information given.

Ex. 1.

| Murata-san | いくらですか？ | *Ikura desu ka?* | How much is it? |
| You | 2千円ぐらいです。 | *Nisen-en-gurai desu.* | About two thousand yen. |

Ex. 2.

| Murata-san | いくらですか？ | *Ikura desu ka?* | How much is it? |
| You | ７千ドルぐらいです。 | *Nanasen-doru-gurai desu.* | About seven thousand dollars. |

Ex. 1.	Ex. 2.	3.	4.
¥1998	$6990	$7997	¥2985
5.	6.	7.	8.
$4989	¥995	¥8999	$3996

◆ Scene 4-2 練習 *Renshuu* Practice

理解練習 *Rikai renshuu* Comprehension practice

4-2-1C What field of study is mentioned? (BTS 6)

The speaker in each audio cue mentions a major or field of study. Write the number of the audio cue next to the matching field of study.

_____ Mathematics   _____ Physics

 Ex. 1 Japan studies   _____ Literature

_____ Religion   _____ Economics

 Ex. 2 Sociology   _____ Linguistics

_____ Engineering

4-2-2C What's being asked? (BTS 9)

Listen to Brian's questions to a salesperson and (a) write the number of the audio cue next to the item that Brian is asking about, then (b) complete the phrase using one of the options below to describe the item that Brian is looking for.

_____ A notebook that's_____

 Ex. 1 Paper that's <u>bigger</u>_____

_____ A pen that's_____

_____ A book that's_____

_____ A bag that's_____

 Ex. 2 An umbrella that's <u>not red</u>_____

_____ A T-shirt that's_____

_____ Cake that's_____

Smaller	Cheaper	Not black	Not white
Not red	Not blue	Bigger	Not so difficult

4-2-3P Confirming something additional (BTS 10)

Kimura-san, who is senior to you, checks on your habits and asks about an additional item. Confirm that the additional item also belongs to your routine.

Ex. 1.

Kimura-san	コーヒーとか、飲みますよね。お茶は？	*Koohii toka, nomimasu yo ne. Ocha wa?*	You drink coffee and the like, right? What about tea?
You	あ、お茶とかも飲みますよ。	*A, ocha to ka mo nomimasu yo.*	Oh, I drink tea and the like, too.

Ex. 2.

Kimura-san	数学が、好きですよね。社会学は？	*Suugaku ga, suki desu yo ne. Shakaigaku wa?*	You like math, right? What about sociology?
You	あ、社会学も好きですよ。	*A, shakaigaku mo suki desu yo.*	Oh, I like sociology, too.

4-2-4P Refusing politely (BTS 12)

When Terada-san, who is slightly senior to you, suggests various activities, refuse politely by indicating that the specified timing won't work.

Ex. 1.	Terada-san	あさって一緒にテニスしませんか？	*Asatte issho ni tenisu shimasen ka?*	How about playing tennis together the day after tomorrow?
	You	あ、あさってですか？すみません。あさってはちょっと‥‥‥	*A, asatte desu ka? Sumimasen. Asatte wa chotto . . .*	The day after tomorrow? I'm sorry. The day after tomorrow won't work.
Ex. 2.	Terada-san	今度の週末、よかったらみんなで何かしませんか。	*Kondo no shuumatsu yokattara minna de nani ka shimasen ka?*	If it's okay, how about doing something with all of us together this coming weekend?
	You	あ、今度の週末ですか？すみません。今度の週末はちょっと‥‥‥	*A, kondo no shuumatsu desu ka? Sumimasen. Kondo no shuumatsu wa chotto . . .*	This coming weekend? I'm sorry. This coming weekend won't work.

4-2 腕試し *Udedameshi* Tryout

Introduce yourself to a Japanese exchange student and find out his/her major.

◆ Scene 4-3 練習 *Renshuu* Practice

理解練習 *Rikai renshuu* Comprehension practice

 4-3-1C What's being asked? (BTS 13)

Listen to Murata-san's question and select the option that best represents what Murata-san wants to know. Pay close attention to the Particles used to mark the topic of the question.

Ex. 1. a. Who is from Canada?

        ⓑ Where is Wang-san from?

Ex. 2. ⓐ Who will make it?

        b. Will Suzuki-san make it or not?

3. a. Who will come?

    b. Is Kawakami-san coming or not?

4. a. Which one is cheap?

    b. Is this a cheap one or not?

5. a. Which bag is new?

    b. Is that bag new or not?

6. a. Which one is difficult?

    b. Is Sakamoto-sensei's difficult or not?

7. a. Which one is expensive?

    b. Is this blue one expensive or not?

8. a. What day is Yamamoto-san?

    b. Who is it tomorrow?

9. a. Which one is old?

    b. Is that one over there old or not?

実演練習 *Jitsuen renshuu* Performance practice

 4-3-2P When does or did it happen? (BTS 20)

Today is Wednesday and Murata-san, your office associate, checks with you about the timing of some activities. Respond by either confirming the day or providing the accurate information.

日 Sun	月 Mon	火 Tue	水 Wed	木 Thu	金 Fri	土 Sat
	4. Buy office supplies	Ex. 2. Study for Japanese Proficiency Exam	**TODAY**	Ex. 1. Go to Aoi Publishing	5. Talk with new clients	
	7. Meet with Shirai-san			3. Start a new project!! 6. Work with Shirai-san		

Ex. 1. Murata-san	今日行きましたか。	*Kyoo ikimashita ka?*		Did you go today?
You	いや、明日行きますよ。	*Iya, ashita ikimasu yo.*		No, I'll go tomorrow.
Ex. 2. Murata-san	昨日勉強しましたか。	*Kinoo benkyoo shimashita ka?*		Did you study yesterday?
You	ええ、昨日しましたよ。	*Ee, kinoo shimashita yo.*		Yes, I studied yesterday.

4-3-3P Implying that there's more going on (BTS 14)

Provide a negative reply to your colleague Yoshida-san's questions, implying that there might be more to the story.

Ex. 1. Yoshida-san	高かったでしょ?	*Takakatta desho?*		It was expensive, right?
You	いや、高くなかったけど……。	*Iya, takakunakatta kedo . . .*		No, it wasn't expensive, but . . .
Ex. 2. Yoshida-san	先生だったでしょ?	*Sensee datta desho?*		It was the teacher, right?
You	いや、先生じゃなかったけど……。	*Iya, sensee ja nakatta kedo . . .*		No, it wasn't the teacher, but . . .

4-3-4P Giving accurate information (BTS 13)

Sakata-san, a friend (junior to you) at Fukuzawa University, has an old list of students who are studying in America. Correct her misconceptions based on the updated chart below.

Student's name	Host university
Takashi Matsuura	Clinton University
Nobuto Ishikawa	UCLA
Noriko Murakami	Peking University
Takayuki Nozawa	Texas Tech University
Saori Taneda	The Ohio State University

Ex. 1.

Sakata-san	村上さんはUCLAですよね。	*Murakami-san wa UCLA desu yo ne.*	Murakami-san is at UCLA, right?
You	あ、いや、北京大学じゃないかな。	*A, iya, Pekin-daigaku ja nai ka na.*	Um, no, isn't she at Peking University?

Ex. 2.

Sakata -san	野沢さんがオハイオ州立大学ですよね。	*Nozawa-san ga Ohaio-shuuritsu-daigaku desu yo ne.*	It is Nozawa-san that's at The Ohio State University, right?
You	あ、いや、種田さんがオハイオ州立大学じゃないかな。	*A, iya, Taneda-san ga Ohaio-shuuritsu-daigaku ja nai ka na.*	Um, no, isn't it Taneda-san that's at The Ohio State University?

◆ Scene 4-4 練習 *Renshuu* Practice

理解練習 *Rikai renshuu* Comprehension practice

4-4-1C What day is it? (BTS 19)

Write the day of the month mentioned in each conversation using Arabic numerals as shown in the example.

Ex. 1. __15__   Ex. 2. __9__   3. _____

    4. _____   5. _____   6. _____

    7. _____   8. _____   9. _____

実演練習 *Jitsuen renshuu* Performance practice

4-4-2P Confirming when the guests came/will come here (BTS 20)

Today is the 19th day of the month. Confirm your teacher's assumption about the guests' arrival day here, using the pattern from the examples.

Ex. 1.	Sakamoto-sensei	明日ですね?	*Ashita desu ne?*	Is it tomorrow?
	You	はい、明日来ます。	*Hai, ashita kimasu.*	Yes, they're coming tomorrow.
Ex. 2.	Sakamoto-sensei	１３日でしたね?	*Juu-san-nichi deshita ne?*	It was the 13th?
	You	はい、１３日に来ました。	*Hai, juu-san-nichi ni kimashita.*	Yes, they came on the 13th.

4-4-3P Telling from when to when (BTS 22)

Respond to your supervisor, Kanda-san, based on the calendars.

114

Ex. 1.

| Kanda-san | いつですか？ | *Itsu desu ka?* | When is it? |
| You | １６日から１９日までです。 | *Juu-roku-nichi kara juu-ku-nichi made desu.* | From the 16th to the 19th. |

Ex. 2.

| Kanda-san | いつですか？ | *Itsu desu ka?* | When is it? |
| You | ７日から１１日までです。 | *Nanoka kara juu-ichi-nichi made desu.* | From the 7th to the 11th. |

Ex. 1.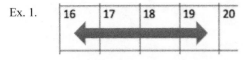

Ex. 2.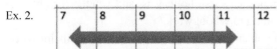

3.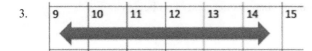

4.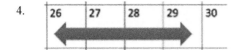

5.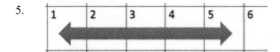

6.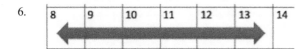

7.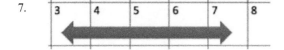

8.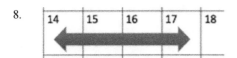

9.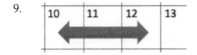

4-4-4P Asking what the alternative is

Respond to your colleague's negative comment by asking by whom, when, or where it will be done.

Ex. 1. Yoshida-san 田中さんはダメですね。 *Tanaka san wa dame desu ne.* Tanaka-san's no good.

You じゃ、誰がしますか。 *Ja, dare ga shimasu ka?* Then who will do it?

Ex. 2. Yoshida-san ２０日はダメですね。 *Hatsuka wa dame desu ne.* The 20th is no good.

You じゃ、何日にしますか。 *Ja, nan-nichi ni shimasu ka?* Then when will (we) do it?

4-4 腕試し *Udedameshi* Tryout

1. Find out what and when the next major Japanese holiday is, and whether or not your Japanese friend/colleague will be coming to school/work.
2. Invite a friend to do something with you and, if s/he accepts, work out details for where and when you will meet.
3. Ask a Japanese exchange student when his/her next class begins and ends.

4-4
れんらく き
連絡来ました?

◆ Scene 4-5 練習 *Renshuu* Practice

理解練習 *Rikai renshuu* Comprehension practice

4-5-1C Waiting for someone (BTS 13, 24)

Circle "who" if the man tells you who waited, or "for whom" if he tells you the person he waited for. Then write the name of the person mentioned in the space provided.

Ex. 1. (who)   for whom   __Tanaka-san__

Ex. 2. who   (for whom)   __Yamamoto-san__

   3. who   for whom   _____-san__

   4. who   for whom   _____-san__

   5. who   for whom   _____-san__

   6. who   for whom   _____-san__

   7. who   for whom   _____-san__

実演練習 *Jitsuen renshuu* Performance practice

4-5-2P Interjecting opinions (BTS 25)

Respond to your colleague by offering your assumption about how easy or difficult the activities must have been, according to the illustrations.

Ex. 1.

| Suzuki-san | 使いましたよ。 | *Tsukaimashita yo.* | I used it! |
| You | そうですか。使いやすかったでしょう。 | *Soo desu ka. Tsukaiyasukatta deshoo.* | Really. I bet it was easy to use, wasn't it. |

Ex. 2.

| Suzuki-san | 作りましたよ。 | *Tsukurimashita yo.* | I made it! |
| You | そうですか。作りにくかったでしょう。 | *Soo desu ka. Tsukurinikukatta deshoo.* | Really. I bet it was hard to make, wasn't it. |

Ex. 1.	Ex. 2.	3.	4.
5.	6.	7.	8.

 ### 4-5-3P Asking questions (BTS 13, 24)

Ask a team member a question based on the context. Then check what you said with the model and listen to her response.

You are wondering:

Ex. 1.	Who will do a certain task.
Ex. 2.	Which of several items would be best (to use).
3.	What she bought at the store.
4.	Which of several items she used.
5.	Who would be best (for a certain task).
6.	What she will study.

4-5 腕試し *Udedameshi* Tryout

1. Ask a friend or colleague about his/her weekly schedule.
2. Find out when the Japanese school year begins and ends.

◆ Scene 4-6 練習 *Renshuu* Practice

理解練習 *Rikai renshuu* Comprehension practice

4-6-1C Naming or counting time? (BTS 29)

Listen to the audio and indicate whether the speaker is naming a point in time or counting time. Then write the time or the amount of time. If you hear something unfamiliar, rely on what you know to choose the correct answer.

Ex. 1.	☒ naming time	☐ counting time	_____9:00_____
Ex. 2.	☐ naming time	☒ counting time	_2 hours 30 minutes_
3.	☐ naming time	☐ counting time	_____
4.	☐ naming time	☐ counting time	_____
5.	☐ naming time	☐ counting time	_____
6.	☐ naming time	☐ counting time	_____
7.	☐ naming time	☐ counting time	_____
8.	☐ naming time	☐ counting time	_____
9.	☐ naming time	☐ counting time	_____

実演練習 *Jitsuen Renshuu* performance practice

4-6-2P Restating to confirm assumptions (BTS 29)

Confirm Tanaka-san's assumptions about when or for how long you did something.

Ex. 1.

Tanaka-san	ちょっと使いましたね。ええと……３時間ですか。	*Chotto tsukaimashita ne. Eeto . . . san-jikan desu ka?*	You used it a bit, didn't you? Um . . . was it three hours?
You	はい、３時間ぐらい使いました。	*Hai, san-jikan gurai tsukaimashita.*	Yes, I used it for three hours.

119

Ex. 2.

| Tanaka-san | ちょっとしましたね。ええ
と‥‥‥１２時ですか。 | *Chotto shimashita ne. Eeto*
. . . juu-ni-ji desu ka? | You did it a bit, didn't
you? Um, was it twelve
o'clock? |
| You | はい、１２時にしました。 | *Hai, juu-ni-ji ni shimashita.* | Yes, I did it at twelve
o'clock. |

3.	4.	5.	6.

 4-6-3P Clarifying what is assumed (BTS 27)

React with a bit of surprise to a club member's assumptions about Wang-san's language
abilities. Based on the illustrations, confirm the language that Wang-san can handle.

Ex. 1.

| Club
member | よくわかりますね。 | *Yoku wakarimasu ne.* | He understands well,
doesn't he. |
| You | え?あの、ワンさん、日本語がわ
かりますか? | *E? Ano, Wan-*
san, nihongo ga
wakarimasu ka? | Huh? Um, does Wang-san
understand Japanese? |

Ex. 2.

| Club member | よく話しますね。 | *Yoku hanashimasu ne.* He speaks well, doesn't he. |
| You | え?あの、ワンさん、英語を話しますか? | *E? Ano, Wan-san, eigo* Huh? Um, does Wang-san *o hanashimasu ka?* speak English? |

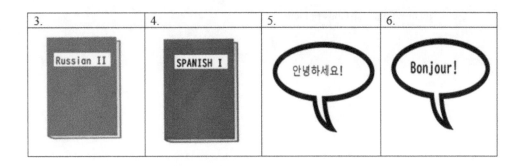

 ## 4-6-4P Indicating the important information (BTS 27)

Initiate the conversation by asking a co-worker a question based on the prompt. The information you are most concerned about is circled in the prompt.

Ex. 1.

| You | 英語は田中さんがわかりますね? | *Eigo wa Tanaka-san ga wakarimasu ne?* | It's Tanaka-san that understands English, right? |
| Morita-san | はい、田中さんがわかります。 | *Hai, Tanaka-san ga wakarimasu.* | Yes, it's Tanaka-san. |

Ex. 2.

| You | 田中さんは英語がわかりますね? | *Tanaka-san wa eigo ga wakarimasu ne?* | It's English that Tanaka-san understands, right? |
| Morita-san | はい、英語がわかります。 | *Hai, eigo ga wakarimasu.* | Yes, it's English. |

Ex. 1. (Tanaka-san) understands English

Ex. 2. Tanaka-san understands (English)

3. Suzuki-san can play (do) (tennis)

4. (Kobayashi-san) needs an umbrella

5. Yoshino-san has a (bicycle)

6. (Ito-san) can do Korean

7. Kato-san understands (Chinese)

8. Morikawa-san needs (a bag)

9. (Yamaguchi-san) understands French

読み練習 *Yomi-renshuu* Reading practice

4-7-1R Reporting where something or someone was or where something was taking place

Circle the appropriate particle for each of the statements.

Ex. 1.	神田さんはオフィス	に・で	いましたけど ……。
Ex. 2.	ミーティングは大学	に・で	ありましたけど ……。
3.	ご飯はアパート	に・で	食べましたけど ……。
4.	クッキーとかケーキはここ	に・で	ありましたけど ……。
5.	ポスターはコピールーム	に・で	作りましたけど ……。
6.	歴史とか文学のクラスは大学	に・で	取りましたけど ……。
7.	クラスメートはクラス	に・で	いましたけど ……。
8.	パソコンはあのお店	に・で	買いましたけど ……。

4-7-2R Expressing or asking about limitation

Choose what fits in each of the statements or questions. You may choose each option once.

a. 大きいの　b. 英語　c. これ　d. 1時間　e. たかし君　f. 数学

Ex. 1.　クラスは＿＿＿f＿＿＿だけです。

Ex. 2.　テニスは＿＿＿d＿＿＿だけしました。

3.　ルームメートは＿＿＿＿＿＿＿だけ来ました。

4.　＿＿＿＿＿＿＿だけですか。韓国語もわかりますか。

5.　大きいかばんは、＿＿＿＿＿＿＿だけですか。

6.　かばんは、この＿＿＿＿＿＿＿だけですか。

4-7-3R Expressing contrast

Choose what fits in each of the statements or questions. You may choose each option once.

| a. 歴史 b. 先生 c. うち d. スーパー e. おととい |
| f. ＣＤ g. 傘 h. 神田さん i. それ j. シャーペン |

1. ＤＶＤはありますが、＿＿＿f＿＿＿はありません。

2. 数学は取りますが、＿＿a＿＿は取りません。

3. かばんはありますが、＿＿＿＿＿＿はないですね。

4. ここでは読みますが、＿＿＿＿＿＿では読みませんよね。

5. 学生は来ますが、＿＿＿＿＿＿は来ませんよ。

6. 寺田さんは遅かったですけど、＿＿＿＿＿＿は遅くなかったですよね。

7. ここの店にはありましたが、あそこの＿＿＿＿＿＿にはありませんでしたよ。

8. きのうはけっこう忙しかったけれど、＿＿＿＿＿＿は全然忙しくなかったですよ。

9. この鉛筆は使いやすいけど、あの＿＿＿＿＿＿は使いにくいですよね。

4-7-4R Asking for information

Match each of the following questions to the appropriate responses.

Ex. 1. ここはどこでしょうか。	＿j＿	a. 「meeting」って言いますよ。
Ex. 2. 専攻は何ですか。	＿d＿	b. ３Ｆじゃないでしょうか。
3. あのパソコンはどうでしょうか。	＿＿＿	c. あの先生ですよ。分かりますか。
4. あれはどなたですか。	＿＿＿	d. 日本語です。
5. この会議は何時から始めましょうか。	＿＿＿	e. 数学でした。
6. 専攻は何でしたか。	＿＿＿	f. ４時半ぐらいからはどうですか。
7. 坂本さんはどちらでしょうか。	＿＿＿	g. 沼田さんじゃないですか。
8. 白井先生はどの先生でしょうか。	＿＿＿	h. 福沢高校じゃなかったでしょうか。
9. 寺田さんはどちらの高校でしたか。	＿＿＿	i. ちょっと使いにくいですよ。
10. 「会議」は英語で何と言いますか。	＿＿＿	j. コロンバスですよ。

4-7-5R Under human control or not

Circle the appropriate particle for each of the questions.

Ex. 1.　　　　だれ　　　　　　　　⓪・を　　　　　しましたか。

Ex. 2.　　　　だれの名前^{なまえ}　　　　が・⓪　　　　　書^かきましたか。

3.　　　　どこ　　　　　　　　　が・を　　　　　作^{つく}りやすいですか。

4.　　　　どのかばん　　　　　が・を　　　　　高^{たか}いですか。

5.　　　　どの先生^{せんせい}の数学^{すうがく}　が・を　　　　　取^とりましたか。

6.　　　　どの公園^{こうえん}　　　　が・を　　　　　きれいですか。

7.　　　　どれ　　　　　　　　　が・を　　　　　できませんでしたか。

8.　　　　どなた　　　　　　　　が・を　　　　　坂本先生^{さかもとせんせい}ですか。

9.　　　　だれのＣＤ　　　　　が・を　　　　　聞^ききましたか。

10.　　　　あの先生^{せんせい}の英語^{えいご}　が・を　　　　　分^わかりましたか？

4-7-6R Preferred word order

Select the preferred word order.

Ex. 1.　(A. 図書館^{としょかん}で　　B. 数学^{すうがく}を　　C. 今日^{きょう}は)

　　　__C__　　__A__　　__B__　勉強^{べんきょう}します。

Ex. 2.　(A. テニスを^{てにす}　　B. 神田^{かんだ}さんは　　C. 3時^じに)

　　　__B__　　__C__　　__A__　します。

3.　(A. 佐藤^{さとう}さんが　　B. 仕事^{しごと}が　　C. 明日^{あした}は)

　　　_____　_____　_____　できますよ。

4.　(A. 2ページ^{ぺえじ}から　　B. あの本^{ほん}は　　C. 34ページ^{ぺえじ}まで)

　　　_____　_____　_____　読^よみました。

5.　(A. 昨日^{きのう}は　　B. 昼^{ひる}ご飯^{はん}も　　C. 朝^{あさ}ご飯^{はん}も)

　　　_____　_____　_____　食^たべませんでした。

6.　(A. あそこまで　　B. ここから　　C. どのぐらい)

　　　_____　_____　_____　かかりますか？

7.　(A. モリス^{もりす}さんは　　B. あのポスター^{ぽすたあ}を　　C. このお店^{みせ} で)

　　　_____　_____　_____　作^{つく}りました。

◆ 書き練習 *Kaki-renshuu* Writing practice

文字練習 *Moji renshuu* Symbol practice

Use the Symbol Practice sheets in Appendix A to practice a hiragana character #46 for Scene 4-7.

 4-7-7W Fill-in-the-blank

Listen to the audio and fill in the blanks with the particles you hear. If there is no particle, put X.

Ex. 1.	だれ	が	しますか。		
Ex. 2.	どこ	で	しますか。		
3.	いつ	_____	しますか。		
4.	どれ	_____	しますか。		
5.	だれ	_____	いいですか。		
6.	どこ	_____	いいですか。		
7.	いつ	_____	いいですか。		
8.	どれ	_____	いいですか。		
9.	どれ	_____	ありますか。		
10.	どこ	_____	ありますか。		
11.	これ	_____	それ	_____	ありますか。
12.	いつ	_____	いつ	_____	しますか。

4-7-8W Sentence completion

Complete the following based on what you hear.

Ex. 1.　これはしますが、あれは<u>しません</u>＿＿＿＿＿＿＿＿＿＿＿＿＿＿＿＿＿＿＿＿＿。

Ex. 2.　あれはしましたが、それは<u>しませんでした</u>＿＿＿＿＿＿＿＿＿＿＿＿＿＿＿＿。

3. それはおいしいですけど、これは＿＿＿＿＿＿＿＿＿＿＿＿＿＿＿＿＿＿＿＿＿＿＿。

4. ここはおいしかったですけど、あそこは＿＿＿＿＿＿＿＿＿＿＿＿＿＿＿＿＿＿＿。

5. このかばんはいいですが、あのかばんは＿＿＿＿＿＿＿＿＿＿＿＿＿＿＿＿＿＿＿。

6. そのＤＶＤはよかったですが、あれは＿＿＿＿＿＿＿＿＿＿＿＿＿＿＿＿＿＿＿＿。

7. ここはきれいですが、あそこは＿＿＿＿＿＿＿＿＿＿＿＿＿＿＿＿＿＿＿＿＿＿＿。

8. あそこはきれいでしたが、そこは＿＿＿＿＿＿＿＿＿＿＿＿＿＿＿＿＿＿＿＿＿＿。

9. ここにはありますが、あそこには＿＿＿＿＿＿＿＿＿＿＿＿＿＿＿＿＿＿＿＿＿＿。

10. 傘^{かさ}はありましたが、かばんは＿＿＿＿＿＿＿＿＿＿＿＿＿＿＿＿＿＿＿＿。

◆ 評価 *Hyooka* Assessment

Answer sheet templates are provided in Appendix B for the Assessment sections.

聞いてみよう *Kiite miyoo* Listening comprehension

Read the context, listen to the audio, and then answer the questions. If you hear something unfamiliar, rely on what you know to choose the correct answer.

1. A man is asking a female colleague about her hotel accommodations.

    a. On what point does the woman agree with the man?
    b. What comment does the woman add?

2. A man asks his colleague about a recent trip.

    a. Where did the woman go?
    b. How does the woman describe that place?
    c. Why does the man thank the woman?

3. A man and a woman are looking at a menu in a café.

    a. What are they trying to decide?
    b. What does the woman suggest?
    c. What is the final decision?

4. Two colleagues are talking in their office.

    a. Who is the man looking for?
    b. How many days will that person be gone?
    c. What additional information does the woman provide?

5. Members of a volunteer organization are talking about a new design for their logo.

    a. What does the man first ask the woman?
    b. What is her response?
    c. What does the man assume about the process?

6. Two members of a community club are talking about an upcoming event.

    a. What does the woman initially ask?
    b. What is the man's response?
    c. What else does the woman find out?

7. Two students are talking at a student orientation.

   a. What is the man's major?
   b. What subjects is the man especially bad at?

8. Two interns are talking about a restaurant.

   a. When did the man go there?
   b. Give details about the restaurant based on what the man says: What's its name? Is it new or old? What kind of cuisine is served? How are the prices?

使ってみよう *Tsukatte miyoo* Dry run

Listen to the audio, and respond based on the context. Then compare what you said to the sample response.

1. Your teacher asks you whether you have been to Hokkaido. Tell him that you went last year.
2. Your colleague suggests buying a new electronic device. Remind him that the one you have (this one) isn't that old.
3. Your teacher mentions a "Professor Sakamoto." Check if he is talking about the very well-known figure in your field by that name.
4. A member of your school activity club is wondering which of the advertisement posters from various years will be good to use in a presentation that you are working on. Suggest (a) the one from the upcoming year; (b) the one from the year before last year; (c) the ones from the Showa era; (d) the ones from the upcoming academic term.
5. Respond to a co-worker with some ambiguity or uncertainty as you share the following information: (a) you are from Canada; (b) tomorrow won't work; (c) the event will be held the day after tomorrow; (d) it's Mr. Anderson who has arrived.

Now it's your turn to start the conversation based on the given context. Listen to how the other person reacts to you. For some items, you may not get a verbal response. If you hear something unfamiliar, rely on what you know to choose the correct answer.

6. You have to finish a project before you go home this evening. Tell your co-worker that you'll be going home late.
7. Tell your teacher that the new poster was a bit hard to read.
8. You are brainstorming about an upcoming event. Pose these questions: (a) from what date to what date it is scheduled; (b) from which day of the week to which day of the week that means; (c) from which time to which time it will be held; and (d) which numbered pieces of equipment (from which number to which number) will be used.

読んでみよう *Yonde miyoo* Contextualized reading

You are reading a text with some help from a furigana-generating website/browser add-on/app, etc. Read the passages below and answer the questions that follow in English.

1. Here is a text message from your supervisor:

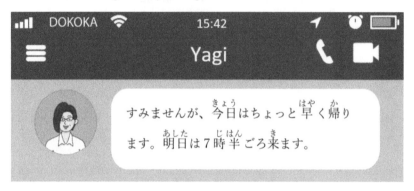

a. Why does the writer apologize?
b. What does the writer tell you about his/her schedule tomorrow?

2. Here are some text messages between two colleagues:

a. What is the topic of these text messages?

b. What does the writer in the first text message ask for confirmation of?

c. Why does the writer of the second text message mention the Nihon Hotel? Why is a meeting mentioned in the second text message?

d. How is the Nihon Hotel described?

3. Here is an email message you received from your instructor about your class:

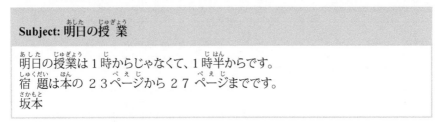

Subject: 明日の授業

明日の授業は1時からじゃなくて、1時半からです。
宿題は本の23ページから27ページまでです。
坂本

a. What does the instructor say about the class time tomorrow?

b. What is the homework assignment?

4. Your coworker Tanaka-san uses an app to add furigana to messages. Here is an email he received:

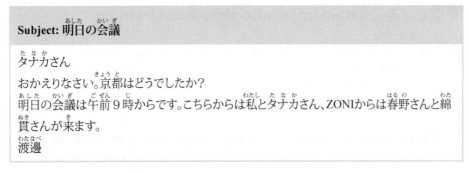

Subject: 明日の会議

タナカさん
おかえりなさい。京都はどうでしたか?
明日の会議は午前9時からです。こちらからは私とタナカさん、ZONIからは春野さんと綿貫さんが来ます。
渡邊

a. Where has Tanaka-san been recently?

b. When will the meeting be held?

c. Who will attend the meeting? Where are they from?

d. Can you guess why Tanaka is written in *katakana*?

5. Here is a text message you received from your classmate:

来学期の韓国語の授業の時間と場所、わかりますか。

a. What does your classmate want to know?

書き取り *Kakitori* Dictation

Listen, imagine the context, repeat silently what you hear, then write it down.

1. _____ 。
2. _____ 。
3. _____ 。
4. _____ 。
5. _____ 。
6. _____ 。
7. _____ 。
8. _____ 。

書いてみよう *Kaite miyoo* Contextualized writing

Consider the context provided and write a note according to the directions.

For all writing tasks below, you need katakana: コピー (noun) "copy, copies," and コピーします (verb) "(make) copies, copy, duplicate." Make sure to use appropriate particles. Write your message horizontally.

1. You are looking at a memo from an assistant that refers to copies he has made. On a sticky note attached to the memo, ask the assistant where the copies are located.

2. You have just made copies for your supervisor. On a sticky note attached to the copied document, tell the supervisor that you made copies of this (document) up to and including page 39 (write "p. 39").

3. On your desk you found a copy of a schedule that seems to be an old version. On a sticky note attached to the copy, ask your assistants who made copies of this (schedule), and when they copied it.

知ってる? *Shitte'ru?* What do you know?

Select the most appropriate option and write the letter in the space on your answer sheet.

1. You've been asked if you made the tarts. You reply:
   いいえ、＿＿＿＿＿でした。*Iie, _____ deshita.* (BTS 1)

   a. 作りません *tsukurimasen*
   b. 作らなかった *tukuranakatta*
   c. 作らない *tsukuranai*

2. You've been asked if the train was early. You reply:

いいえ、＿＿＿＿＿＿なかったです。 *Iie, ＿＿＿＿＿nakatta desu.* (BTS 1)

  a. 早い *hayai*

  b. 早く *hayaku*

  c. 早かった *hayakatta*

3. You ask if someone's major wasn't linguistics.

言語学＿＿＿＿ですか。 *Gengogaku ＿＿＿＿desu ka.* (BTS 1)

  a. なかった *nakatta*

  b. じゃなかった *ja nakatta*

  c. じゃありません *ja arimasen*

4. You've been asked about dinner. You reply:

＿＿＿＿＿＿でした。 ＿＿＿＿＿＿ *deshita.* (BTS 1)

  a. おいしくありません *Oishiku arimasen*

  b. 食べなかった *Tabenakatta*

  c. よくなかった *Yoku nakatta*

5. You give your colleague an idea of the kinds of things you ate at the party.

クッキー＿＿＿パイを食べました。 *Kukkii ＿＿＿ pai o tabemashita.* (BTS 8, 11)

  a. だけ *dake*

  b. とか *to ka*

  c. あと *ato*

6. You're not entirely certain that something is true.

本当＿＿＿。 *Hontoo ＿＿＿.* (BTS 2)

  a. でしょう *deshoo*

  b. ですよ *desu yo*

  c. ですね *desu ne*

7. You plan to go home late tonight.

今晩＿＿＿帰ります。 *Konban ＿＿＿kaerimasu.* (BTS 3)

  a. 遅い *osoi*

  b. 遅かった *osokatta*

  c. 遅く *osoku*

8. Which of the following represents *yonhyakuman gosen-en?* (BTS 4)

    a. ¥ 450,000

    b. ¥ 405,000

    c. ¥ 4,005,000

9. You waited about 40 minutes for your friend.

    ４０分_____待ちました。*Yonjuppun _____machimashita.* (BTS 5)

    a. ぐらい *gurai*

    b. ごろ *goro*

    c. には *ni wa*

10. You ask the salesperson if they only have Japanese teas. (BTS 9)

    a. 日本のはお茶だけですか。*Nihon no wa ocha dake desu ka.*

    b. お茶は日本のだけですか。*Ocha wa nihon no dake desu ka.*

    c. 日本のお茶はこれだけですか。*Nihon no ocha wa kore dake desu ka.*

11. The interviewer asks you what you studied in college. You reply:

    社会学、言語学、_____日本語を勉強しました。*Shakaigaku, gengogaku, _____ nihongo o benkyoo shimashita.* (BTS 11)

    a. だけ *dake*

    b. も *mo*

    c. あと *ato*

12. By ending a sentence with けど *kedo* or が *ga,* you sound as if you're _____. (BTS 12)

    a. familiar with the situation

    b. hedging your response

    c. completely certain

13. You ask the manager who will do the buying.

    だれ_____買いますか。*Dare _____ kaimasu ka.* (BTS 13, 24)

    a. が *ga*

    b. は *wa*

    c. を *o*

14. You wonder which cookie is delicious.

    どれ_____おいしいでしょうか。*Dore _____oishii deshoo ka.* (BTS 13, 24)

    a. が *ga*

    b. は *wa*

    c. を *o*

15. You point out that it was Ms. Terada who baked all the cakes.

寺田さん＿＿＿＿全部作りました。

Terada-san ＿＿＿＿ zenbu tsukurimashita. (BTS 13, 24)

   a. を *o*

   b. は *wa*

   c. が *ga*

16. Compared to other subjects, you think that physics is very difficult.

物理＿＿＿＿とっても難しい。*Butsuri ＿＿＿＿tottemo muzukashii.* (BTS 13)

   a. が *ga*

   b. は *wa*

   c. を *o*

17. You ask your *koohai* in the office informally about yesterday's meeting.

30分だけじゃ＿＿＿＿＿？ *Sanjuppun dake ja ＿＿＿＿＿?* (BTS 14)

   a. なかった *nakatta*

   b. ないです *nai desu*

   c. ありません *arimasen*

18. Which of the following time words would occur with particle に *ni* to indicate when something took place? (BTS 20)

   a. 先月 *sengetsu*

   b. 三月 *sangatsu*

   c. 先学期 *sengakki*

19. You want to politely contradict the new intern about who's teaching the seminar tomorrow.

あしたは木村先生＿＿＿＿＿＿か。*Ashita wa Kimura-sensei ＿＿＿＿＿＿ ka?* (BTS 21)

   a. でしょう *deshoo*

   b. じゃなかったです *ja nakatta desu*

   c. 教えません *oshiemasen*

20. You're certain that the class begins at 4:00 and not 3:00.

4時＿＿＿＿＿ですよ。*Yoji ＿＿＿＿＿ desu yo.* (BTS 22)

   a. に *ni*

   b. まで *made*

   c. から *kara*

21. Your friend asked you to check on when the library closes tonight. You reply:

今晩は１０時半_____です。 *Konban wa juujihan _____ desu.* (BTS 22)

    a. まで *made*

    b. から *kara*

    c. に *ni*

22. You want to know which computer your coworker plans to use.

どれ_____使いますか。 *Dore _____ tsukaimasu ka.* (BTS 24)

    a. は *wa*

    b. を *o*

    c. が *ga*

23. You've been asked which one you want to buy. You reply:

これ_____お願いします。 *Kore _____ onegai shimasu.* (BTS 24)

    a. は *wa*

    b. が *ga*

    c. を *o*

24. You're convinced that it's pretty hard to understand the boss' Japanese.

_____分かりにくいですよ。 _____ *wakarinikui desu yo.* (BTS 26)

    a. あまり *Amari*

    b. ちょっと *Chotto*

    c. わりと *Wari to*

25. You don't think it's going to be easy to make the new program.

ちょっと_____ですねえ。 *Chotto _____ desu nee.* (BTS 25)

    a. 作りやすい *tsukuriyasui*

    b. 作りやすくない *tsukuriyasuku nai*

    c. 作りにくくない *tsukurinikuku nai*

26. Classifier completion: (BTS 29)

四 *Yon-*

    a. 時間 *jikan*

    b. 週間 *shuukan*

    c. 年 *nen*

27. 九 *Kyuu-*

    a.   時間 *jikan*

    b.   日 *nichi*

    c.   年 *nen*

28. You've been asked how long you'll lay over at the airport. You reply:
_____ぐらいです。 _____ *gurai desu.* (BTS 29)

    a.   二時間 *Nijikan*

    b.   ２時 *Niji*

    c.   日曜日 *Nichiyoobi*

29. Which of the following are true regarding the differences between spoken and written Japanese? (BTL 1)

    a.   が *ga* is more common in spoken language; けれど、けども、けれども *keredo, kedomo, keredomo* are more common in writing.

    b.   けど is more common in spoken language; けれど、けども、けれども are more common in writing.

    c.   じゃ is a written form while では is a spoken form.

30. Japanese input on a computer _____. (BTL 3)

    a.   uses a Japanese keyboard
    b.   requires a Japanese operating system
    c.   can be done using romanization

第 5 幕
Act 5

お願いしてもいいですか。

May I ask a favor of you?

聞くは一時の恥、聞かぬは一生の恥
To ask may lead to shame for a moment,
but not to ask leads to shame for a lifetime.

◆ Scene 5-1 練習 Practice

理解練習 Comprehension practice

5-1-1C Identifying 〜て forms (BTS 1)

Select the meaning of the 〜て form you hear from the options below. You will not use every option.

Ex. 1. __h__   Ex. 2. __o__   3. _____   4. _____   5. _____

6. _____   7. _____   8. _____   9. _____   10. _____

a. write	b. expensive	c. do	d. make	e. speak
f. listen	g. hurry	h. return	i. come	j. new
k. use	l. fast	m. wait	n. buy	o. finish

実演練習 Performance practice

5-1-2P Taking up an offer (BTS 2)

Respond positively to Ikebe-san (a new part-time worker) when she offers to do various things.

Ex. 1.
Ikebe-san	手伝いましょうか。	Shall we/I help?
You	じゃあ、手伝ってください。すみません。	Then please help. Thanks.

Ex. 2.
Ikebe-san	Tシャツ作りましょうか。	Shall we/I make T-shirts?
You	じゃあ、作ってください。すみません。	Then please make (it). Thanks.

5-1-3P Either will be fine. (BTS 2)

Your work associate presents two alternatives. Respond that either will be fine.

Ex. 1.

| Tanaka-san | 今日しましょうか。明日しましょうか。 | Shall we/I do it today or tomorrow? |
| You | 今日でも明日でもいいですよ。 | Either today or tomorrow will be fine. |

Ex. 2.

| Tanaka-san | 大きく書きましょうか。小さく書きましょうか。 | Shall I draw it big or small? |
| You | 大きくても小さくてもいいですよ。 | Either big or small is fine. |

5-1-4P Suggesting that it probably won't make a difference (BTS 2)

Respond to a suggestion from a member of your project group that it probably won't make a difference whether or not you do what she suggests.

Ex. 1.

| Kawata-san | 今日しましょうか。 | Shall we/I do it today? |
| You | 今日してもしなくても同じでしょう。 | Either doing it today or not will probably be the same. |

Ex. 2.

| Kawata-san | 会いましょうか。 | Shall we/I meet them? |
| You | 会っても会わなくても同じでしょう。 | Either meeting them or not will probably be the same. |

◆ **Scene 5-2 練習 Practice**

理解練習 Comprehension practice

5-2-1C What does Sakamoto-san want to do? (BTS 4)

Select from the options below what Sakamoto-san (the female speaker) wants permission to do. If you hear something unfamiliar, rely on what you know to choose the correct answer.

Ex. 1. __h__   Ex. 2. __c__   3. _____   4. _____   5. _____

6. _____   7. _____   8. _____

a. ask a question	b. bring a cell phone	c. use something
d. not come in April	e. not hurry	f. come again next year
g. take about 3 months	h. make it the day after tomorrow	

実演練習 Performance practice

5-2-2P Giving the benefit of the doubt (BTS 3)

Your colleague is wondering about something. If she is wrong, correct her, assuming that she actually has access to the same information; otherwise, go along with her in wondering about the situation.

Ex. 1.	$1 = ¥107	
Akiyama-san	今1ドル108円ぐらいですかねえ。	I wonder if a dollar is about 108-yen.
You	いや、107円ぐらいでしょう？	No, it's about 107-yen, don't you know.
Ex. 2.	??	
Akiyama-san	来週の会議、どの会議室ですかねえ。	In which conference room will next week's meeting be?
You	どの会議室でしょう。	Which conference room, I wonder.

　　3. Hitory; 4. Not Room 206; 5. Test on Thursday; 6. ??

5-2-3P Denying permission (BTS 2, 4)

When a junior colleague asks permission not to do something, politely tell him to do it.

Ex. 1.

| Tomoda-san | これ、しなくてもいいですか。 | Is it okay if I don't do this? |
| You | いや、やっぱりしてください。すみません。 | No, as you might expect, please do it. Sorry. |

Ex. 2.

| Tomoda-san | あの大きいの、使わなくてもいいですか。 | Is it okay if I don't use the big one? |
| You | いや、やっぱり使ってください。すみません。 | No, as you might expect, please use it. Sorry. |

5-2-4P Doing it and going home (BTS 4)

When a junior colleague asks for confirmation that you did something yesterday, tell her that you did it and went home.

Ex. 1.

| Ikebe-san | 食べましたね? | You ate (some), right? |
| You | はい、食べて帰りました。 | Yes, I ate (some) and went home. |

Ex. 2.

| Ikebe-san | 会議しましたね? | You held a meeting, right? |
| You | はい、会議して帰りました。 | Yes, I held a meeting and went home. |

5-2 腕試し Tryout

Ask a superior, such as a boss or a teacher, for permission to do something. For example, you could ask if it is all right to drink water in class, if it is all right to leave early (e.g., because you're not feeling well), or if it is all right to submit an assignment before the assigned due date.

◆ **Scene 5-3 練習 Practice**

理解練習 Comprehension practice

5-3-1C How many are there? (BTS 6)

In each conversation identify the quantity of items.

Ex. 1. <u>seven</u>   Ex. 2. <u>two</u>   3. _____   4. _____

5. _____   6. _____   7. _____

5-3-2C How polite is it? (BTS 5)

Listen to the four requests and rank them from most polite to least polite. (Keep in mind that the least polite request is still polite.)

Most polite: _____

Next most polite: _____

Third most polite: _____

Least polite: _____

実演練習 Performance practice

5-3-3P Agreeing and requesting (BTS 5, 6)

Express agreement with the quantity your team member suggests and politely request that she take care of it.

Ex. 1.

Takagi-san	買って来ますけど、6つぐらいがいいでしょうか。	I'll go buy them, but would about 6 do?
You	そうですね。6つぐらい買って来ていただけますか?	Yes, would you kindly go and buy about 6?

144

Ex. 2.

| Takagi-san | コピーして来ますけど、２０枚ぐらい がいいでしょうか。 | I'll go make copies, but would about 20 sheets do? |
| You | そうですね。２０枚ぐらいコピーして 来ていただけますか? | Yes, would you kindly go and make about 20 copies? |

5-3 腕試し Tryout

Make a polite request to a superior, such as a boss or a teacher. For example, you could ask your teacher to look over an assignment you completed.

5-3

お願いしてもいいですか。

145

◆ **Scene 5-4 練習 Practice**

理解練習 **Comprehension practice**

5-4-1C What's going on? (BTS 8, 9)

Select the option that corresponds to what the speaker says.

Ex. 1. __b__   Ex. 2. __a__   3. _____   4. _____   5. _____
6. _____   7. _____   8. _____   9. _____   10. _____

Ex. 1.   a. I went to the car.
          b. I went by car.
Ex. 2.   a. I saw the university.
          b. I saw it at the university.
   3.   a. I waited in the train.
          b. I waited for the train.
   4.   a. I went to the bank.
          b. I went from the bank to somewhere else.
   5.   a. I drew it using a pencil.
          b. I drew a picture of a pencil.
   6.   a. I studied in the hospital.
          b. I studied about the hospital.
   7.   a. I came to Fukuzawa University.
          b. I came from Fukuzawa University.
   8.   a. I talked on the telephone.
          b. I talked about the telephone.
   9.   a. I saw the supermarket.
          b. I saw it at the supermarket.
  10.   a. I came to the post office.
          b. I came from the post office.

5-4-2C What's the location?

Select the location that is being discussed from the options below.

Ex. 1. __b__   Ex. 2. __j__   3. _____   4. _____   5. _____
6. _____   7. _____   8. _____   9. _____   10. _____

a. bank	b. bookstore	c. supermarket	d. hospital	e. convenience store
f. park	g. classroom	h. library	i. train station	j. meeting room

実演練習 Performance practice

5-4-3P Stating your destination (BTS 7, 8)

Your co-worker identifies a place where you can get something done or find something you need. Tell her that you are going to make a quick run to that place.

Ex. 1.

Sato-san	これ、銀行でできますよ。	You can get this done at a bank, you know.
You	じゃあ、ちょっと銀行まで行ってきます。	Then, I'll make a quick run to the bank.

Ex. 2.

Sato-san	これ、駅の本屋にありますよ。	They have this at the bookstore in the station, you know.
You	じゃあ、ちょっと駅の本屋まで行ってきます。	Then, I'm make a quick run to the bookstore in the station.

5-4-4P Suggesting a means for an action (BTS 9)

When your team member proposes an activity, suggest how to do it based on the illustrations.

Ex. 1.

Takahashi-san	大阪の病院まで行きましょう。	Let's go to a hospital in Osaka.
You	じゃあ、バスで行きましょう。	Then let's go by bus.

Ex. 2.

Takahashi-san	本屋で買いましょう。	Let's buy it at a bookstore.
You	じゃあ、クレジットカードで買いましょう。	Then let's buy it with a credit card.

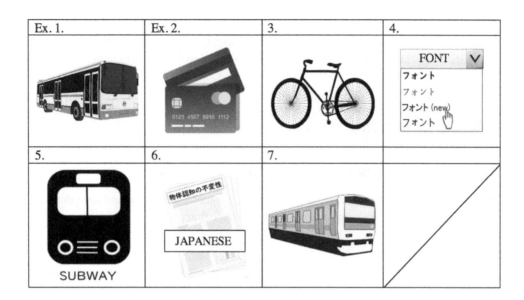

Ex. 1.	Ex. 2.	3.	4.
			FONT ∨ フォント フォント フォント (new) フォント
5.	6.	7.	
SUBWAY	物体認知の不変性 JAPANESE		

5-4 腕試し Tryout

Ask someone how s/he gets to work or school every day and how long it takes.

◆ Scene 5-5 練習 Practice

理解練習 Comprehension practice

 5-5-1C What's going on? (BTS 12)

Select the option that corresponds to what the speaker says.

Ex. 1. __a__   Ex. 2. __b__   3. _____   4. _____   5. _____

6. _____   7. _____   8. _____   9. _____   10. _____

Ex. 1.   a. I got a present from my friend.
          b. I got a present because we're friends.
Ex. 2.   a. I came from Fukuzawa University.
          b. I came because it's Fukuzawa University.
3.   a. I did it starting on page 5.
          b. I did it because it's only 5 pages.
4.   a. I'm going home at 4 o'clock.
          b. It's 4 o'clock, so I'm going home.
5.   a. I won't be going from the dorm.
          b. I won't be going because it's a dorm.
6.   a. I heard it from Yamashita-san.
          b. I heard it, because it's Yamashita-san.
7.   a. We're starting on Thursday.
          b. It's Thursday, so we're going to start.
8.   a. It's about 20 minutes from the university.
          b. It's the university, so it's about 20 minutes.
9.   a. We'll do it starting on the 2nd.
          b. We'll do it because it's only 2 days.
10.   a. I borrowed it from the teacher.
          b. I borrowed it because she's a teacher.

5-5

お願いしてもいいですか。

149

理解実演練習 Comprehension and performance practice

5-5-2CP What would you say? (BTS 10)

Imagine what you would say in each situation and say it aloud. Then listen to the audio and select the one that best matches what you came up with.

Ex. 1. You would like to meet with Yagi-san, the division chief, and she has said that tomorrow at 10:00 a.m. works. Let her know that you will visit her at that time.

a._____ b._____ c.___○___

Ex. 2. Tomoda-san, a new intern, has just told you that he will attend a certain function tomorrow. Confirm this information to make sure you understood correctly.

a._____ b._____ c._____ d.___○___

3. You are meeting Yamamoto-san, a client of your company, for the first time. When she asks, tell her that you came to Japan last month.

a._____ b._____ c._____ d._____

4. You are wondering when Yagi-san, the division chief, will be going to the US.

a._____ b._____ c._____ d._____

5. Yamamoto-san, a client of your company, has asked if you will be visiting him next Monday. Tell him that you will be there next Monday at 3:00 p.m.

a._____ b._____ c._____

6. Ask Tomoda-san, the newly hired intern, if he's going to Kyoto for Golden Week.

a._____ b._____ c._____

5-5-3CP Inviting Sakamoto-sensei to events (BTS 10)

Invite Sakamoto-sensei, your Japanese language teacher, to the activities listed below. Listen to how she responds and indicate whether she will (○) or will not (✗) attend.

Ex. 1.

You	先生、よろしければ先生もあさっての発表にいらっしゃってください。	Professor, if it's all right, please come to the presentation the day after tomorrow.
Sakamoto-sensei	あさってですか？伺います。	The day after tomorrow? Yes, I'll come.

Ex. 2.

You	先生、よろしければ先生も午後のプレゼンにいらっしゃってください。	Professor, if it's all right, please come to the presentation in the afternoon.
Sakamoto-sensei	今日の午後ですか？午後はちょっと……。	In the afternoon today? The afternoon won't work.

Ex. 1.	Ex. 2.	3.
Award Announcement Ceremony in 2 days!	Presentation PM Session	Reception Next week
4.	**5.**	**6.**
Presentation Thursday!	Concert in October	Reception This academic term: TBD

Ex. 1. ___○___   Ex. 2. ___✗___   3. _____   4. _____   5. _____
6. _____

実演練習 Performance practice

 5-5-4P Reassuring someone that you'll be there by the specified time (BTS 10, 12)

When Watanabe-san, a business client, tells you when an event begins, reassure him that you'll be there by that time.

Ex. 1.

Watanabe-san	うちの発表は 16 時 20 分からですが・・・・・・。	The announcement/presentation is from 4:20 p.m. . . .
You	わかりました。では、16 時 20 分までに参りますから。	All right. Then, I'll be there by 4:20 p.m., so. . . .

Ex. 2.

Watanabe-san	会議は 6 日からですが・・・・・・。	The conference starts on the 6th. . . .
You	わかりました。では、6 日までに参りますから。	All right. Then, I'll be there by the 6th so. . . .

お願いしてもいいですか。

5-5 腕試し Tryout

1. Thank a superior or someone you don't know well for something that s/he did for you.
2. Ask someone, such as a teacher or your boss, what the deadline is for a certain task (by when it should be done).

お願いしてもいいですか。

◆ Scene 5-6 練習 Practice

理解練習 Comprehension practice

5-6-1C What are the appointment details? (BTS 15, 16)

Kato-san, the first speaker, is making appointments with various people. Complete the table below with the missing information about who he will meet, when and where. If you hear something unfamiliar, focus on what you know to determine the correct answer.

	Whom?	When?	Where?
Ex. 1.	Professor Sakamoto	After the second class	Classroom
Ex. 2.	Kawamura-san, a senior student	Before the linguistics class	In front of the library
3.			In Professor Shirai's office
4.			In the classroom
5.	Nakamura-san, a student organization leader		
6.	Suzuki-san, a classmate		In a lounge on the ____ floor

実演練習 Performance practice

5-6-2P Agreeing with the description of an outcome (BTS 14)

Agree with your teammate's description, and add that it is the result of a change.

Ex. 1.

Watanabe-san	難しいですねえ、このプレゼン。	It's difficult, isn't it—this presentation.
You	そうですねえ。すごく難しくなりましたねえ。	Yes. It's become very difficult, hasn't it!

5-6
お願いしてもいいですか。

153

Ex. 2.

| Watanabe -san | おもしろいですねえ、あの社会学の 授業。 | It's interesting, isn't it—that sociology class. |
| You | そうですねえ。すごくおもしろくなり ましたねえ。 | Yes. It's become very interesting, hasn't it! |

5-6-3P Requesting a classmate to help (BTS 5, 15)

A classmate who is slightly older than you asks you about an activity. Politely request that he do it together with you.

Ex. 1.

| Yoshida-san | 練習しますか？ | Are you going to practice? |
| You | はい、あの、すみませんけど、一 緒に練習していただけませんか。 | Yes, um, sorry, but would you practice together with me? |

Ex. 2.

| Yoshida-san | 時間決めますか？ | Are you going to decide on the time? |
| You | はい、あの、すみませんけど、 一緒に決めていただけませんか。 | Yes, um, sorry, but would you decide together with me? |

5-6 腕試し Tryout

Make an appointment with a superior, such as your teacher or your boss.

お願いしてもいいですか。

読み練習 Reading practice

Read all items silently, then re-read them out loud.

5-7-1R Introducing oneself

Who is doing this self-introduction? Write down the person's name.

Ex. 1.	セスです。よろしく。	Seth
Ex. 2.	スーです。どうぞよろしく。	Sue
3.	はじめまして。キアです。どうぞよろしく。	_____
4.	キース・オスカーです。よろしくお願_{ねが}いします。	_____
5.	はじめまして。カーク・アーサーです。よろしくお願_{ねが}いします。	_____

5-7-2R Seeking information about things and events

Match the questions on the left with the appropriate response on the right.

Ex. 1.	あのノートはどこですか。	c	a. ¥50,000 ぐらいじゃないでしょうか。
Ex. 2.	テニスはいつしますか。	d	b. コーニーさんじゃありませんか。
3.	あのコートはだれのでしょうか。	___	c. アニタさんのデスクにありますよ。
4.	このツアーはいくらでしょうか。	___	d. あしたの4時_じです。
5.	このウイスキーはどこのでしょうか。	___	e. ネイトさんのじゃありませんか。
6.	あしたのコーチはどなたですか。	___	f. そうですね。¥35,000 ぐらいじゃありませんか。
7.	このスーツはなかなかいいですね。いくらぐらいでしょうか。	___	g. テネシーのです。おいしいでしょう？

5-7-3R Correcting information

Fill in the blank by choosing the appropriate option from the selection below.

> a. カナダ　b. チーズケーキ　c. エドガーさん　d. ツアーガイド　e. ツアー

Ex. 1.　ゲイツさんはドイツじゃなくて、＿＿a＿＿じゃないですか。

Ex. 2.　あの＿＿＿e＿＿＿はギニアじゃなくて、ケニアじゃありませんか。

3.　あしたのデザートはアイスじゃなくて、＿＿＿＿＿＿＿じゃないでしょうか。

4.　＿＿＿＿＿＿＿はサウスダコタじゃなくて、ノースダコタじゃないでしょうか。

5.　シカゴの＿＿＿＿＿＿＿はダニーさんじゃなくて、デニスさんじゃありませんか。

5-7-4R Asking for permission

Fill in the blank by choosing the appropriate option from below.

> a. スキー　b. サッカー　c. クッキー　d. スタート　e. カット

Ex. 1.　アーサーさんと＿＿＿a＿＿＿に行ってもいいですか。

Ex. 2.　ここ、＿＿＿e＿＿＿してもよろしいですか。

3.　あしたみんなで＿＿＿＿＿＿＿してもいいでしょうか。

4.　この＿＿＿＿＿＿＿、いただいてもよろしいでしょうか。

5.　あのツアーはあさってから＿＿＿＿＿＿＿してもいいでしょうか。

5-7-5R Thank-you memos

Fill in the blank by choosing the appropriate option from below.

> a. 教えて　b. 決めて　c. 連れていって　d. 持ってきて　e. 呼んで　f. 見て

Ex. 1. 宿題を＿＿＿＿f＿＿＿くださってありがとうございました。

Ex. 2. ケーキを＿＿＿＿d＿＿＿くださってありがとうございました。

3. 友だちも＿＿＿＿＿＿くださってありがとうございました。

4. 英語を＿＿＿＿＿＿くださってありがとうございました。

5. 会議の日を＿＿＿＿＿くださってありがとうございました。

6. 銀行まで＿＿＿＿＿くださってありがとうございました。

5-7-6R Identifying an odd item

Underline the item that does not belong to the list.

Ex. 1.	スキー	テニス	サッカー	タクシー
Ex. 2.	チーズ	ココア	クッキー	ケーキ
3.	タクシー	セーター	スカート	ソックス
4.	コネチカット	サウスダコタ	テキサス	シカゴ
5.	ドイツ	カナダ	チケット	ガーナ
6.	ザック	テッド	ダニー	デイジー

5-7

お願いしてもいいですか。

文字練習 Symbol practice

Use the Symbol Practice sheets in Appendix A to practice *katakana* characters #1-25 for Scene 5-7.

5-7-7W Making a shopping list

Create a shopping list based on the voice mail from your host mother.

> - スイスチーズ
> -
> -

5-7-8W Writing down names

You are a new exchange student. Listen to your new classmates introduce themselves, and write down their full names in katakana.

Ex. 1.	ノア・オットー
Ex. 2.	アニタ・ウッド
3.	
4.	
5.	

◆ 評価 Assessment

Answer sheet templates are provided in Appendix B for the Assessment sections.

聞いてみよう Listening comprehension

Read the context, listen to the audio, and then answer the questions. If you hear something unfamiliar, rely on what you know to choose the correct answer.

1. Takashi has borrowed several books from Amy.

   a. What is Takashi asking?
   b. How does Amy respond?
   c. What request does Amy make?

2. Kanda-san has been asked by a salesperson to try a new game that's very challenging.

   a. What is Kanda-san's concern?
   b. How does the salesperson try to reassure Kanda-san?
   c. Does this reassure Kanda-san?

3. Sakamoto-sensei has some work to be done and approaches Kanda-san.

   a. When does Sakamoto-san ask Kanda-san to start the work?
   b. By what time does Sakamoto-san want the work done?
   c. How much of the work does Sakamoto-san ask Kanda-san to do by this time?
   d. How does Kanda-san respond to Sakamoto-san's request?

4. Yamamoto-san from Aoi Printing has brought a new poster that was just printed to Yagi-san.

   a. What does Yamamoto-san express thanks for?
   b. What does Yamamoto-san ask Yagi-san to do?
   c. What does Yagi-san think of the poster?

5. Sasha is getting ready for a meeting when Kanda-san stands up and heads toward the door.

   a. Where is Kanda-san going? Where is it located?
   b. What does Sasha tell Kanda-san about the meeting?
   c. What might Sasha be concerned about?
   d. How does Kanda-san reassure Sasha?

6. Sasha is checking with Kanda-san about an event that she is organizing.

   a. What assumption does Sasha make about Kanda-san?
   b. When will the event occur?

お願いしてもいいですか。

c. What does Kanda-san ask Sasha?

d. How does Sasha respond to Kanda-san's request?

7. Brian is talking to a classmate in his Japanese class.

 a. What are they talking about? How has it changed?

 b. What does Brian's classmate suggest?

 c. What does Brian suggest?

 d. What does Brian want to know?

 e. How does Brian's classmate respond? What does he add about today and tomorrow?

8. Sakamoto-sensei has distributed a worksheet to everyone in Brian's class.

 a. What does Sakamoto-sensei ask the students?

 b. What does Sakamoto-sensei tell the class to do? By when?

 c. What does Sakamoto-sensei say about #8?

 d. Why is the student relieved?

9. Sasha and Kanda-san just played a game of tennis.

 a. What does Kanda-san say about Sasha's tennis ability?

 b. What does Sasha thank Kanda-san for?

10. An office intern is preparing a poster for an upcoming meeting.

 a. What does the intern ask?

 b. Why does Sasha apologize?

 c. What is Sasha referring to when she says こっち?

 ## 使ってみよう Dry run

Listen to the audio and respond based on the context. Then compare what you said to the sample response.

1. An intern is asking about doing something. Respond affirmatively by telling him to do it (a through e).

2. Yamamoto-san, your company's client, asks if he can come back again. Respond affirmatively by telling him to come back again.

3. An office associate suggests two possible co-workers for the next project. Respond that either would be fine.

4. Yamamoto-san, your company's client, asks when you came to Japan. Respond that you arrived last month.

5. An office associate is wondering if a new item is needed. Respond that it will probably be okay whether it is new or not.

6. An intern points out that a reference book is outdated. Ask her to go to the book store in 3 丁目 and buy a new one.

7. An office associate wonders if she should ask Tomoda-san. Respond that it probably won't make a difference (i.e., will be the same) whether she asks him or not.

8. On your way to visit a client one of the interns points out that you don't have much time. Agree and respond that you should hurry.

9. Your friend is very impressed with the beautiful waterfall that you've taken him to see, as you predicted he would be. Agree with him in a way that shows you thought he would feel that way.

10. A friend asks why you threw something away. Explain that it's because (a) it's old; (b) you don't use it; (c) it's a bit small; (d) it's not interesting; (e) it's not pretty; (f) it's the one from last week.

11. Your office associates asks about the number of tables in the conference room. Respond that there are two large ones and three small ones.

Now it's your turn to start the conversation based on the given context. Listen to how the other person reacts to you. For some items, you may not get a verbal response. If you hear something unfamiliar, rely on what you know to choose the correct answer.

12. Without implying that there are other options ask an office associate if it's all right to (a) write in pencil; (b) go to the bank; (c) think (about it); (d) buy a new one; (e) use this; (f) turn it in tomorrow; (g) take a look.

13. While implying that there are other options, ask an office associate if it's all right to (a) do it tomorrow; (b) begin right now; (c) eat this part; (d) show her something; (e) make a new one; (f) ask one thing; (g) request her to do something; (h) borrow this book.

14. A rather sensitive issue has come up. Politely request the *senpai* in charge to call in the division manager.

15. An office associate will be using the conference room for a meeting. Politely ask her to be finished by 3 o'clock.

16. You are going to visit a client with a *senpai* from the office. Ask how you will get there.

17. You just finished practicing tennis at a community center with a *senpai* from your school's tennis club. Thank her for practicing here with you.

18. Ask the intern to go to the factory and borrow a new one from Nakatani-san tomorrow, because it's too late today.

19. Comment to Shirai-san on how much Ichiro-kun has grown.

20. You are talking to a teacher about meeting sometime. Ask if it's all right if it's after your second period class.

読んでみよう Contextualized reading

Read the information and answer the questions that follow in English.

1. Here's a list of study abroad participants from the US at a Japanese university.

氏名 (しめい)　　　　　出身地 (しゅっしんち)
1. キース・ウッド　　　テキサス
2. アニタ・クック　　　テネシー

3. ケイト・ゲイツ　　　　　　　　　サウスダコタ
4. アイザック・カーター　　　　　　コネチカット

   a. How many female students are on the list?
   b. Where is Keith from?
   c. Who is from the East Coast of the US?
   d. What is Gates-san's first name? Where is she from?

2. Here is an online search result for men's clothes.

メンズ			
Vネックセーター ☆☆☆☆☆ ¥2,800	コート ☆☆☆☆☆ ¥8,000	スーツ ☆☆☆☆☆ ¥6,800	ソックス ☆☆☆☆☆ ¥680

   a. What is the most expensive item?
   b. What is the cheapest item?
   c. What type of sweater is on sale?

 ## 書き取り Dictation

Listen, imagine the context, repeat silently what you hear, then write it down.

1. _____ 。

2. _____ 。

3. _____ 。

4. _____ 。

5. _____ 。

6. _____ 。

7. _____ 。

8. _____ 。

書いてみよう Contextualized writing

Compose a note according to the directions.

1. You are leaving a pamphlet for a group tour on the desk of your supervisor, Cook-san. On a sticky note attached to the pamphlet, politely invite her to join you by saying "Please come to this tour, if you would like."

2. You are organizing a reception. Write a brief memo to West-san, your client, and politely ask him to come by taxi tomorrow.

3. You found a notebook in a conference room. Leave it on Carter-san's desk with a sticky note asking if this notebook isn't his.

Act 5 お願いしてもいいですか。

知ってる? What do you know?

Select the most appropriate option and write the letter on your answer sheet.

1. You invite another student to come to your party.
   _____ください。(BTS 1, 2)

   a. きて
   b. きいて
   c. かいて

2. You wish to ask for permission to go home early today.
   今日早く_____。(BTS 2, 4)
   a. 帰って大丈夫でしょう
   b. 帰ってください
   c. 帰ってもいいでしょうか

3. You intend to buy something no matter the price.
   _____高くなくても買います。(BTS 2)

   a. 高くても
   b. 安くても
   c. 高くて

4. Which of the following is <u>not</u> used to express manner? (BTS 2)

   a. The -ku form of adjectives
   b. The -te form of adjectives
   c. The -te form of verbs

5. You think the apartment is clean and assume that your friend does too.
   すごくきれい_____ (BTS 3)

   a. だった?
   b. でしょう?
   c. でしょうか。

6. You suggest that you have ramen before going home and studying. (BTS 4f)

   a. ラーメンを食べて、家へ帰って、勉強しましょう。
   b. 家へ帰って、ラーメンを食べて、勉強しましょう。
   c. 勉強して、ラーメンを食べて、家へ帰りましょう。

7. You tell another student that the test was really hard and you didn't do well.
   ＿＿＿＿＿＿＿＿ できませんでした。(BTS 4f)

   a. 難^{むずか}しい
   b. 難^{むずか}しくて
   c. 難^{むずか}しかった

8. You ask your advisor politely if she can bring something to the meeting tonight. (BTS 5)
   持^もってきて＿＿＿＿＿＿＿＿＿＿＿＿＿。

   a. ください
   b. お願^{ねが}いします
   c. いただけませんか

9. You tell your roommate that you'll go look at the apartment next door and then be right back.
   ちょっと＿＿＿＿＿＿。(BTS 7)

   a. 見^みています
   b. 見^みてきます
   c. 見^みていきます

10. You tell your office mate that you'll email Tamura-san.
    田村^{たむら}さん＿＿＿＿メールします。(BTS 8)

    a. を
    b. に
    c. で

11. You tell your friend you'll go to the reception by car.
    車^{くるま}＿＿＿＿行^いきます。(BTS 9)

    a. に
    b. へ
    c. で

12. You ask your homestay mother if it's okay to bring your friend to the party.
    友達^{ともだち}を＿＿＿＿もいいでしょうか。(BTS 7)

    a. 連^つれていって
    b. 持^もってきて
    c. 連^つれてきて

Act 5 お願いしてもいいですか。

13. You ask your supervisor if she'll be coming to the conference hotel tomorrow too.

明日^{あす}も＿＿＿＿＿＿＿＿＿＿＿か。(BTS 10)

    a. 参^{まい}ります

    b. いらっしゃいます

    c. 伺^{うかが}います

14. Politeness levels in Japanese conversations are ＿＿＿＿＿＿. (BTS 10)

    a. determined by such factors as formality and status

    b. fixed and pre-determined

    c. reserved for special occasions

15. You thank your coworker for helping you with a task.

＿＿＿＿＿＿＿ありがとうございます。(BTS 11)

    a. 手伝^{てつだ}って

    b. 手伝^{てつだ}ってください

    c. 手伝^{てつだ}ってくださって

16. You tell your friend why you're going to play a certain game this week.

先週^{せんしゅう}＿＿＿＿＿から、今週^{こんしゅう}は。(BTS 12)

    a. しなかったです

    b. しなかった

    c. しませんでした

17. ございます is the polite equivalent of ＿＿＿＿＿.(BTS 10)

    a. あります

    b. います

    c. します

18. You ask your assistant to get the job done by 4:00.

4時^じ＿＿＿＿してください。(BTS 13)

    a. に

    b. まで

    c. までに

19. You think that a certain restaurant has gotten expensive.

あのレストランは高^{たか}く＿＿＿＿＿＿＿ねぇ。(BTS 14)

    a. なりました

    b. なくなりました

    c. なかったです

20. You realize that Japanese class has really gotten to be a lot of fun!

    _____ねえ。(BTS 14)

    a. 面白<ruby>面白<rt>おもしろ</rt></ruby>かったです
    b. 面白<ruby>面白<rt>おもしろ</rt></ruby>くなります
    c. 面白<ruby>面白<rt>おもしろ</rt></ruby>くなりました

21. Long vowels are represented in katakana by _____. (BTL 2)

    a. doubling the vowel symbol
    b. using a small X before the vowel symbol
    c. using the symbol ー after the vowel symbol

22. When a word is borrowed into Japanese _____. (BTL 3)

    a. both the meaning and the pronunciation may change
    b. the pronunciation stays the same, but the meaning may change
    c. the meaning stays the same, but the pronunciation may change

23. When words are borrowed into Japanese, syllables that end in consonants _____. (BTL 4)

    a. acquire a vowel
    b. become /n/
    c. double the consonant

24. Syllables with an /r/ such as *car* and *fur* are likely to_____. (BTL 5)

    a. become short /a/ syllables
    b. occur with other consonants
    c. become long /a/ syllables

25. In borrowed words, syllables that begin with /w/ become _____. (BTL 8)

    a. long vowels
    b. ウ plus a vowel
    c. short vowels

26. Voiced consonants include _____. (BTL 9)

    a. /t/ and /d/
    b. /g/, /z/, and /d/
    c. /k/, /s/, and /t/

27. In katakana, double consonants are represented by _____ . (BTL 10)

    a. a reduced size katakana ツ
    b. a reduced size hiragana つ
    c. doubling the consonant symbol

いつもお世話になっております。

We always appreciate your helpfulness.

明日の百より今日の五十

A bird in the hand is worth two in the bush.

◆ Scene 6-1 練習 Practice

理解練習 Comprehension practice

6-1-1C Ongoing action vs. resulting state (BTS 1)

For each utterance, mark whether the 〜ています form is indicating an ongoing action (OA) or a resulting state (RS).

Ex. 1.	☐ OA	☒ RS
Ex. 2.	☒ OA	☐ RS
3.	☐ OA	☐ RS
4.	☐ OA	☐ RS
5.	☐ OA	☐ RS
6.	☐ OA	☐ RS
7.	☐ OA	☐ RS
8.	☐ OA	☐ RS
9.	☐ OA	☐ RS
10.	☐ OA	☐ RS
11.	☐ OA	☐ RS
12.	☐ OA	☐ RS
13.	☐ OA	☐ RS
14.	☐ OA	☐ RS

6-1-2C What's going on? (BTS 2, 3)

Select the option that corresponds to what the speaker says.

Ex. 1. __a__	Ex. 2. __b__	3. _____	4. _____	5. _____
6. _____	7. _____	8. _____	9. _____	10. _____

Ex. 1. a. I've already borrowed it.
   b. I still have it.

Ex. 2. a. I'm not looking at it anymore.
   b. I still haven't looked at it.

3. a. Yuya isn't my roommate anymore.
   b. Yuya still isn't my roommate.

4. a. Mizuno-sensei's new book is already available.
   b. Mizuno-sensei's new book is still available.

5. a. It's okay now.
   b. It's still okay.

6. a. I don't get it anymore.
   b. I still don't get it.

7. a. We don't have any anymore.
   b. We still don't have any.

8. a. I still don't need that.
   b. I don't need that anymore.

9. a. We aren't practicing anymore.
   b. We haven't practiced yet.

10. a. It's too late.
    b. It's soon enough.

実演練習 Performance practice

6-1-3P Responding negatively to "yet" questions (BTS 2, 3)

When a *koohai* at work asks you if you have or haven't done something yet, respond with "no," according to the pattern.

Ex. 1.

Tomoda-san	もうしましたか。	Did you do it yet?
You	いや、まだしていません。	No, I haven't done it yet.

Ex. 2.

Tomoda-san	まだしていませんね?	You haven't done it yet, right?
You	いや、もうしましたよ。	No, I already did it.

6-1-4P Apologizing for an assignment not yet completed (BTS 1, 3)

When your supervisor asks about a task, apologize and tell her that you haven't done all of it. Add that you'll do it right away.

Ex. 1.

Takeda-san	レセプションのプログラム、だいたい決めました？	Did you put together most of the reception program?
You	あ、すみません。まだ全部決めてません。すぐやります。	Oh, sorry. I haven't worked all of it out yet. I'll get to it right away.

Ex. 2.

Takeda-san	プレゼンのスライド、全部できました？	Did you get all the presentation slides done?
You	あ、すみません。まだ全部できてません。すぐやります。	Oh, sorry. They're not all done yet. I'll get to it right away.

6-1 腕試し Tryout

1. Ask a Japanese acquaintance who has a hobby how long he or she has been pursuing it.
2. Have a short self introduction ready so that when the opportunity presents itself, you can give it. You may have to alter details to match different contexts.

◆ **Scene 6-2 練習 Practice**

理解練習 Comprehension practice

6-2-1C Where is it? (BTS 8)

In each conversation the woman explains where something is by using a reference point. Connect the reference point with the associated location.

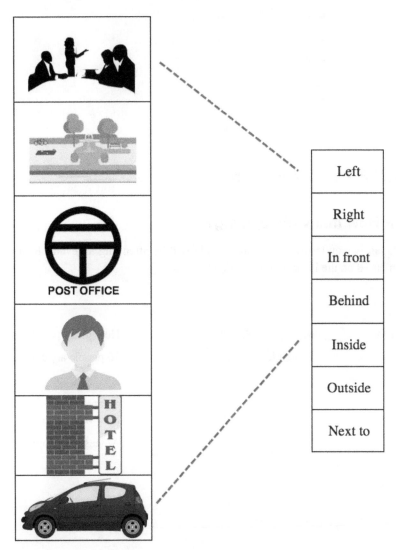

いつもお世話になっております。

173

6-2-2C Point in time or amount of time? (BTS 9)

Mark the appropriate option to indicate whether a point (P) in time or an amount (A) of time is mentioned.

Ex. 1.	☐ P	☒ A
Ex. 2.	☒ P	☐ A
3.	☐ P	☐ A
4.	☐ P	☐ A
5.	☐ P	☐ A
6.	☐ P	☐ A
7.	☐ P	☐ A
8.	☐ P	☐ A
9.	☐ P	☐ A
10.	☐ P	☐ A
11.	☐ P	☐ A

実演練習 Performance practice

 ## 6-2-3P How many are coming?

Yoshida-san is wondering how many people will be attending an event. Respond to her question based on the information provided.

Ex. 1.

Yoshida-san	何人来ますか。	How many people are coming?
You	10人来ます。	10 people are coming.

Ex. 2.

Yoshida-san	何人来ますか。	How many people are coming?
You	１７人は来ます。	At least 17 people are coming.

Ex. 1.	Ex. 2.	3.	4.
	+ ??	+ ??	
5.	6.	7.	8.
	+ ??		

 6-2-4P Where is it? (BTS 8)

Kanda-san is looking for an item. Suggest where it might be based on the information provided.

Ex. 1.

Kanda-san	あのう、財布がちょっと . . .	Um, my wallet is kind of . . .
You	財布ですか。車の中じゃないですか。	Your wallet? Isn't it in the car?

175

Ex. 2.

Red

| Kanda-san | あのう、車が . . . ええと . . . | Um, my car . . . uh . . . |
| You | 車ですか。あの赤い車の後ろのじゃないですか。 | Your car? Isn't it the one behind that red car? |

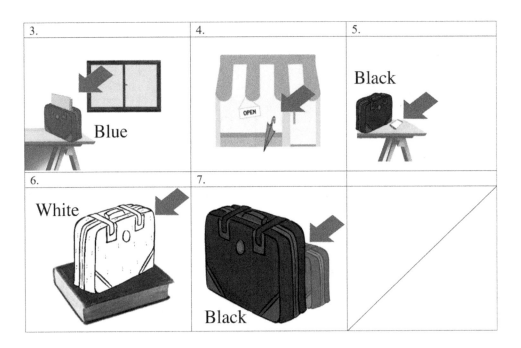

6-2 腕試し Tryout

Introduce yourself to someone you haven't met before. Try to give a more detailed introduction than you have previously.

◆ Scene 6-3 練習 Practice

理解練習 Comprehension practice

 6-3-1C More or already? (BTS 2, 12)

In each utterance, you will hear the word もう. Mark whether it means "more" or "already."

Ex. 1.	☒ More	☐ Already
Ex. 2.	☐ More	☒ Already
3.	☐ More	☐ Already
4.	☐ More	☐ Already
5.	☐ More	☐ Already
6.	☐ More	☐ Already
7.	☐ More	☐ Already
8.	☐ More	☐ Already

 6-3-2C Who is it? (BTS 13)

Sasha is going to meet someone she doesn't know at the train station. Match the person with his/her picture based on Kanda-san's description.

Ex. 1. __b__   Ex. 2. __g__   3. _____

4. _____   5. _____   6. _____

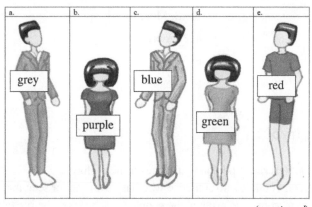

(continued)

177

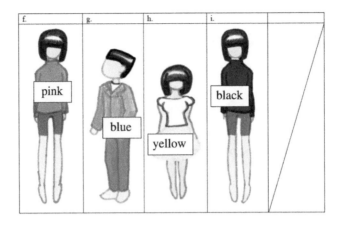

実演練習 Performance practice

 ### 6-3-3P Asking someone to buy more (BTS 12)

When the intern tells you there isn't a lot of a certain item, ask him to buy some more, based on the information given.

Ex. 1.

| Tomoda-san | 青いペンはあまりないですね。 | We don't have many blue pens. |
| You | じゃ、もう２０本買ってください。 | Then please buy 20 more. |

Ex. 2.

| Tomoda-san | お茶はあまりないですね。 | We don't have much tea. |
| You | じゃ、もっと買ってください。 | Then please buy some more. |

Ex. 1. 20 more	Ex. 2. More
3. 15 more	4. 30 more
5. More	6. 5 more
7. More	8. 10 more

6-3 腕試し Tryout

1. Ask someone to describe a person you've never met before.
2. Describe a person you know to someone who has never met or seen that person before.
3. Take a photo of a group, and arrange the people (in Japanese!) before taking the photo.

178

◆ Scene 6-4 練習 Practice

理解練習 Comprehension practice

6-4-1C Listening for contact information (BTS 14)

Write down the contact information that Otani-sensei gives you over the telephone.

Name: Otani _____

Office room number: _____

Office phone number: _____

Mobile phone number: _____

Email-address: _____

実演練習 Performance practice

6-4-2P Confirming a change (BTS 16)

A client notices a change in your office. Acknowledge the change.

Ex. 1.

| Eguchi-san | 電話番号、新しいですね。 | The phone number is new, isn't it? |
| You | あ、はい。電話番号が新しくなりまして……。 | Well, yes. The phone number is new . . . |

Ex. 2.

| Eguchi-san | 入り口、後ろですか? | Is the entrance in the back? |
| You | あ、はい、入り口が後ろになりまして ……。 | Well, yes. The entrance is now in the back . . . |

6-4 腕試し Tryout

1. Introduce yourself to someone in a formal setting and exchange *meishi* with that person.
2. Ask for someone's contact information.
3. Give someone your contact information.

いつもお世話になっております。

◆ **Scene 6-5 練習 Practice**

理解練習 Comprehension practice

 6-5-1C What's going on? (BTS 19)

In each of the following sets, you will hear two different utterances said by Mori-san. For each set, match the utterance with the most appropriate context.

Ex. 1-1. ⓐ/ b   a. An office worker comments about airfares to Vietnam.

Ex. 1-2. a /ⓑ   b. An office worker was surprised to hear that Mori-san won't go on a trip.

   2-1. c / d   c. An acquaintance at a reception has gone back for a third helping of dumplings. Mori-san is guessing that they are delicious.

   2-2. c / d   d. Mori-san is wondering whether something on the menu at a restaurant will be tasty or not.

   3-1. e / f   e. A friend has commented that Mori-san doesn't seem to be making any progress on the homework she's been working on for two hours.

   3-2. e / f   f. A classmate from school has asked Mori-san what she thinks about a homework assignment.

   4-1. g / h   g. Mori-san would like to look at something an office associate is holding.

   4-2. g / h   h. A friend is offering Mori-san an expensive-looking gift and she wants to make sure that it's really alright for her to accept it.

実演練習 Performance practice

 6-5-2P Explaining that you want to (BTS 19, 20)

You are talking to an office associate, who has just heard that you won't be doing something. Explain that you want to, but (won't be able to).

Ex. 1.

Tomoda-san	行かないんですか？レセプション。	You're not going?—the reception.
You	行きたいんですけど ……。	I do want to go, but . . .

Ex. 2.

Tomoda-san	しないんですか?発表。	You're not going to do it?—the presentation.
You	したいんですけど ……。	I do want to do it, but . . .

 6-5-3P Offering to be the one to do it (BTS 21)

You and Shirai-san, your company's client, are discussing who will do various tasks. Offer to be the one to do a certain task, based on the information provided. Then listen to Shirai-san's response.

Ex. 1.

You	じゃ、私がお話ししますから。	Then I'll speak (to him), so . . .
Shirai-san	申し訳ありません。	Sorry (to make you do that).

Ex. 2.

You	じゃ、私が伺いますから。	Then I'll visit (you), so . . .
Shirai-san	すみません。よろしくお願いいたします。	Thank you.

Ex. 1. Offer to speak (to Shirai-san's boss).

   3. Offer to assist (Shirai-san).

   5. Offer to be the one to write (an announcement).

   7. Offer to be the one to wait (for someone).

   9. Offer to be the one to meet (someone).

Ex. 2. Offer to visit (Shirai-san).

   4. Offer to be the one to make it.

   6. Offer to show it (to Shirai-san's boss).

   8. Offer to be the one to do it.

  10. Offer to be the one to invite (someone).

 6-5-4P Using polite language (BTS 21)

For each of the following, say something that would be appropriate for the given context.

	You are talking to:	You want to:
Ex. 1-a.	an office associate	arrange for a time to talk (about something that may be complicated or serious).
Ex. 1-b.	an office associate	talk about something that should not take much time.

2-a.	mayor of the city, to whom you've just been introduced	introduce yourself as someone who works for Ogaki Shokai. (The sample will use Sasha Morris's name.)
2-b.	a new intern at the company where you work	introduce yourself as a full-time employee. (The sample will use Sasha Morris's name.)
3-a.	division chief	have the division chief look over your work for the task you've just completed.
3-b.	division chief	have the division chief bring an item the two of you have been looking at to a meeting with a client tomorrow.
3-c.	an office intern	have the intern make twenty copies of the document you are holding.
4-a.	Yamamoto-san, a client	offer to be the one to make the poster that the two of you have been talking about.
4-b.	an office intern	offer to be the one to write the report for the division manager.
5-a.	a superior	say that you liked the food that the superior offered to you.
5-b.	a superior	exclaim that the food the superior offered to you and that you just ate tasted absolutely amazing.

6-5 腕試し Tryout

Make an appointment with a superior, such as a boss or a teacher.

◆ Scene 6-6 練習 Practice

理解練習 Comprehension practice

 6-6-1C Identifying question word + か & も (BTS 18, 22)

You will hear a question word +か or も in each of your teammate's statements. Which of the four options is its English equivalent?

Ex. 1.	__a__	a. Always	b. Sometimes	c. Everyone	d. Nobody
Ex. 2.	__c__	a. Everyone	b. Nobody	c. Everywhere	d. Nowhere
3.	_____	a. Everyone	b. Nobody	c. Everything	d. One of these
4.	_____	a. Many	b. Some	c. One	d. None
5.	_____	a. Everyone	b. Some one	c. Everything	d. Something
6.	_____	a. Any day	b. No day	c. Everywhere	d. Nowhere
7.	_____	a. Everyone	b. No one	c. Rarely	d. Never
8.	_____	a. Many	b. Some	c. Only one	d. None
9.	_____	a. Everything	b. Something	c. One thing	d. Nothing
10.	_____	a. Everything	b. Something	c. One thing	d. Nothing
11.	_____	a. Every day	b. Never	c. Every one	d. Nobody
12.	_____	a. Everywhere	b. Somewhere	c. Nowhere	d. Never
13.	_____	a. Everyone	b. No one	c. One of the two	d. Neither
14.	_____	a. Some	b. One of the two	c. Both	d. Many
15.	_____	a. Everything	b. Something	c. None of these	d. One of these
16.	_____	a. Everyone	b. One person	c. Both people	d. No one
17.	_____	a. All	b. Something	c. One	d. None
18.	_____	a. All the time	b. Some time	c. Both times	d. Never
19.	_____	A. Some	b. Both	c. One	d. None
20.	_____	A. Everybody	b. Somebody	c. Both	d. Nobody

実演練習 Performance practice

 6-6-2P This one's better. (BTS 24)

Answer a fellow student's questions based on the illustrations.

6-6

いつもお世話になっております。

Ex. 1.

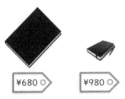

| Ai | どっちの方が高いですか。 | Which one is more expensive? |
| You | 小さい方が高いですね。 | The small one is more expensive. |

Ex. 2.

| Ai | どっちの方がオススメですか。 | Which one would you recommend? |
| You | ラーメンの方がオススメですね。 | Ramen is my recommendation. |

3.

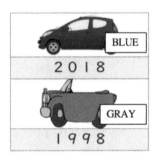

4.

5.

6.

7.

6-6-3P I'll have this. (BTS 28)

You are at a restaurant. When a waiter presents you with drink options, indicate which one you will have, based on the illustration.

Ex. 1.

Waiter	ジュースはパイナップルとグレープフルーツがございますが‥‥‥。	The juices we have are pineapple and grapefruit.
You	じゃ、パイナップルにします。	Then I'll have pineapple.

Ex. 2.

Waiter	ノンアルコールの飲み物はコーヒーとお茶とお水がございますが‥‥‥。	The non-alcoholic beverages we have are coffee, tea, and water.
You	じゃ、お水にします。	Then I'll have water.

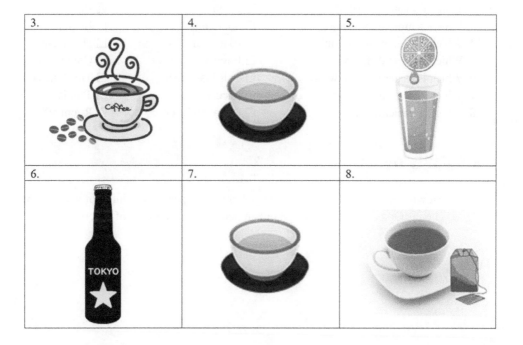

6-6

いつもお世話になっております。

6-6-4CP Which one? (BTS 24)

Ask a fellow student a "which" question based on the information provided. Then mark the option that he responds with.

Ex. 1.

You	水曜日と木曜日と、どちらの方がいい？	Which is better, Wednesday or Thursday?
Hiroshi	水曜日かなあ。	Maybe Wednesday.

Ex. 2.

You	うどんとラーメンと、どちらの方が好き？	Which do you like better, udon or ramen?
Hiroshi	僕は東京の人だからラーメンの方が好き。	I'm from Tokyo, so I like ramen better.

Ex. 1. Which is better	☒ Wednesday	☐ Thursday
Ex. 2. Which do you like better	☐ Udon	☒ Ramen
3. Which is more interesting	☐ Sociology	☐ Literature
4. Which do you want to drink	☐ Black tea	☐ Oolong tea
5. Which is more difficult	☐ English	☐ Chinese
6. Which is easier to write with	☐ This black pen	☐ This blue pen
7. Which has cheaper tickets	☐ Soccer	☐ Tennis
8. Which is easier to use	☐ Room 507	☐ Room 509

6-6 腕試し Tryout

Go out to eat with someone. Before ordering, ask the other person's opinion of what might be a good choice. Or ask for an opinion about an item you are thinking of ordering.

読み練習 Reading practice

Read all items silently, process their meaning, and then read them again out loud.

6-7-1R Ordering food

Underline the type of food that is ordered.

Ex. 1.	パスタをください。	<u>Meal</u>	Drink	Dessert
Ex. 2.	カプチーノをください。	Meal	<u>Drink</u>	Dessert
3.	チーズバーガーを１つください。	Meal	Drink	Dessert
4.	ハム＆エッグとピーチパイをください。	Meal	Drink	Dessert
5.	アイスコーヒーを１つと、ホットコーヒーを２つください。	Meal	Drink	Dessert

6-7-2R Verifying where people are from

Write down the person's name and where s/he is from.

Ex. 1.	スミスさんはネバダですね？	Smith	Nevada
Ex. 2.	トーマスさんはオランダでしょうか。	Thomas	Netherlands
3.	ベネットさんはミネソタからですね？	_____	_____
4.	バーニーさんはミシシッピでしょうか。	_____	_____
5.	マッケンタイヤーさんはアイルランドでしょう？	_____	_____
6.	バーナードさんはウエストバージニアからですね？	_____	_____

6-7-3R Asking for permission

What kind of permission is being sought?

Ex. 1.　これ、コピーしてもいいですか。　　　　　　making copies of this (thing)

Ex. 2.　アップロードしてもいいでしょうか。　　　　　　uploading

　　3.　あしたスタートしてもよろしいですか。　　_____

　　4.　テストはあしたじゃなくてもいいでしょうか。　_____

　　5.　アルバイトのトレーニングはあさってして　　　_____
　　　　もよろしいでしょうか。　　　　　　　　　　　_____

6-7-4R Politely indicating where people are

Write down the person's name and where s/he is.

Ex. 1.　ロペスさんはユタにいらっしゃいます。　　　　Lopez　　　　Utah

Ex. 2.　スミスさんはハワイにいらっしゃいます。　　　Smith　　　Hawaii

　　3.　ルイスさんはコロラドにいらっしゃいます。　_____

　　4.　トーマスさんはシアトルにいらっしゃいます。　_____

　　5.　スコットさんはロサンゼルスにいらっしゃい　_____
　　　　ます。

　　6.　ガルシアさんはワシントンＤＣにいらっし　　_____
　　　　ゃいます。

　　7.　エドワーズさんはケンタッキーにいらっしゃ　_____
　　　　います。

　　8.　トンプソンさんはアーカンソーにいらっしゃ　_____
　　　　います。

　　9.　ロドリゲスさんはペンシルベニアにいらっし　_____
　　　　ゃいます。

　10.　ゴンザレスさんはサンフランシスコにいらっ　_____
　　　　しゃいます。

　11.　ルーズベルトさんはミズーリのセントルイ　　_____
　　　　スにいらっしゃいます。

　12.　アンダーソンさんはオレゴンのポートランド　_____
　　　　にいらっしゃいます。

いつもお世話になっております。

6-7-5R Making requests

What request is being made?

Ex. 1. メモしてください。	__e__	a. design a poster
Ex. 2. リサイクルしてください。	__g__	b. backup the data
3. メールをチェックしてください。	_____	c. download (it) from a website
4. ポスターのデザインをお願い できますか。	_____	d. copy a schedule
5. すみませんが、コメントをいただけますか。	_____	e. take a memo
6. データをバックアップしていただけますか。	_____	f. give a comment
7. このサイトからダウンロードしていただけ ますか。	_____	g. recycle (it)
8. あのデータをコンピューターにインプット してください。	_____	h. check into a hotel
9. あしたは４：３０ PMにホテルにチェックイ ンしてください。	_____	i. cancel a campus tour
10. すみませんが、あしたのキャンパスツアー をキャンセルしていただけますか。	_____	j. check email
11. すみませんが、あさってのスケジュールをコ ピーしていただけないでしょうか。	_____	k. input data on a computer

6-7-6R Stating what people are doing right now

Write down who is doing what.

Ex. 1.	アルバイトは今スケジュールを コピーしています。	part-time worker _____ making copies of the schedule
Ex. 2.	ジョーンズさんは今レシートをチェック しています。	Jones-san _____ checking a receipt
3.	キャンベルさんは今あそこでジョギング しています。	_____ _____
4.	ジョンソンさんは今図書館で勉強して います。	_____ _____
5.	チャールズさんは今ネットでニュース を見ています。	_____ _____

6-7

いつもお世話になっております。

189

6. スチュワートさんは今ロビーでヒューさ
   んと話しています。　　　　　　　＿＿＿＿＿＿＿＿＿＿＿＿
   　　　　　　　　　　　　　　　　　　＿＿＿＿＿＿＿＿＿＿＿＿

7. ネルソンさんは今テレビのドキュメンタ
   リーを見ています。　　　　　　　　＿＿＿＿＿＿＿＿＿＿＿＿
   　　　　　　　　　　　　　　　　　　＿＿＿＿＿＿＿＿＿＿＿＿

8. リチャードソンさんは今レストランでラ
   ンチを食べています。　　　　　　　＿＿＿＿＿＿＿＿＿＿＿＿
   　　　　　　　　　　　　　　　　　　＿＿＿＿＿＿＿＿＿＿＿＿

9. ハリスさんは今コンビニでジュースとチ
   ョコレートを買っています。　　　　＿＿＿＿＿＿＿＿＿＿＿＿
   　　　　　　　　　　　　　　　　　　＿＿＿＿＿＿＿＿＿＿＿＿

10. ホワイトさんは今コンピュータのデータ
    をバックアップしています。　　　　＿＿＿＿＿＿＿＿＿＿＿＿
    　　　　　　　　　　　　　　　　　＿＿＿＿＿＿＿＿＿＿＿＿

11. ジャクソンさんは今ニューヨークのホテ
    ルでインタビューをしています。　　＿＿＿＿＿＿＿＿＿＿＿＿
    　　　　　　　　　　　　　　　　　＿＿＿＿＿＿＿＿＿＿＿＿

6-7-7R Identifying an odd item

Underline the item that does not belong in the list.

Ex. 1.	デパート	スーパー	コンビニ	<u>インターネット</u>
Ex. 2.	バスケットボール	サイクリング	<u>ジャケット</u>	スノボ
3.	ミュージカル	ニューヨークステーキ	シーフードサラダ	パスタ
4.	マサチューセッツ	ニュージャージー	ジョージア	シンガポール
5.	イギリス	サンフランシスコ	フランス	スペイン
6.	ブライアン	ジョージ	ビバリー	ジャック

書き練習 Writing practice

文字練習 Symbol practice

Use the Symbol Practice sheets in Appendix A to practice *katakana* characters #26–46 for Scene 6-7.

6-7-8W Checking if something has been done already

Write a response that you haven't done it yet.

いつもお世話になっております。

Ex. 1.　a. あのレストランはもうオープンしましたか。

　　　　b. いえ、まだ<u>オープンしていません</u>。

Ex. 2.　a. このパンフレットはもうコピーしましたか。

　　　　b. いえ、<u>まだコピーしていません</u>。

　　3.　a. あのデータはもうアップしましたか。

　　　　b. いえ、まだ_____。

　　4.　a. もうブライアンさんにメールしましたか。

　　　　b. いえ、まだ_____。

　　5.　a. このレッスンはもうカバーしましたか。

　　　　b. いえ、まだ_____。

　　6.　a. あのポスターはもうプリントしましたか。

　　　　b. いえ、まだ_____。

　　7.　a. メールはもうチェックしましたか。

　　　　b. いえ、まだ_____。

 ## 6-7-9W Getting to know new people

Four international students have just arrived at Fukuzawa University. Write down their names, hometowns, and hobbies in katakana.

	Name	Hometown	Hobby
Ex. 1.	ヒュー・ジャクソン	イギリス（ロンドン）	スポーツ（バレーボール）
Ex. 2.	ソーニャ・ロドリゲス	プエルトリコ	アニメ
3.			
4.			

いつもお世話になっております。

Answer sheet templates are provided in Appendix B for the Assessment sections.

聞いてみよう Listening comprehension

Read the context, listen to the audio, and then answer the questions. If you hear something unfamiliar, rely on what you know to choose the correct answer.

1. Suzuki-san and her brother are looking at a photograph that was taken at the welcome party for Brian at the aikido school where she and Brian train.

   a. What does Suzuki-san's brother want to know about the photo?
   b. What is Suzuki-san's response? What reason does she give for her response?

2. Suzuki-san shows her brother another photograph, taken on the same occasion.

   a. Who is being discussed?
   b. Where is this person located in this picture?
   c. What does Suzuki-san's brother think about this person's nationality?
   d. How does Suzuki-san explain the situation?
   e. What does Suzuki-san's brother ask related to aikido?
   f. What is Suzuki-san's response? What information does she add to qualify her response?

3. Shirai-san and Sasha are talking after exchanging business cards at a reception.

   a. What does Shirai-san initially tell Sasha?
   b. Why is Shirai-san surprised at Sasha's response?
   c. How does Sasha know Brian? Provide details.
   d. To what extent are Brian and Sasha currently in contact? How long has this been the case?

4. Kanda-san is having difficulty reaching someone on the phone.

   a. Who is Kanda-san trying to reach? Where does this person work?
   b. How did Sasha obtain this person's contact information?
   c. Why is Kanda-san having difficulty reaching this person?
   d. What additional information does Sasha provide to explain the situation?

5. Kanda-san and Sasha are talking about a meeting they attended earlier in the day.

   a. What does Kanda-san think went well?
   b. How does Sasha feel about it?
   c. What reason does Kanda-san give for his opinion?

6. Sasha asks Kanda for permission.

   a. What is Sasha asking permission to do? Provide details.
   b. Why is Sasha asking permission to do this?
   c. Why didn't Sasha schedule her appointment after work?
   d. What was Kanda-san's mistaken assumption?

7. Kanda-san and Sasha are confirming details about a dinner appointment they have with a client.

   a. When is the dinner appointment?
   b. What detail does Sasha check on?
   c. What is "Midori" in relation to the dinner appointment? What other meanings of "Midori" are mentioned?
   d. Where is the restaurant located?

8. Sasha and Kanda-san are attending a dinner that their client is hosting at a Korean BBQ restaurant.

   a. What does the client encourage Sasha to do?
   b. Why does Sasha refuse?
   c. What is the client's concern?
   d. How does Sasha respond to this concern?

9. Yagi-bucho asks Kanda-san to look at a document.

   a. What does Yagi-bucho want Kanda-san to do?
   b. What is Kanda-san's question?
   c. What timeline does Yagi-bucho give Kanda-san?

10. Kanda-san and Sasha are talking about a poster for an upcoming event.

    a. What is Kanda-san asking?
    b. What is Sasha's initial response?
    c. What reason does Sasha give for thinking this way?
    d. What is Sasha's concern?
    e. Does Sasha approve or disapprove of Kanda-san's suggestion?

 ## 使ってみよう Dry run

For each of the following, listen to the audio and respond to what was said based on the context.

1. You are speaking to an office associate. Murata-san is currently (a) writing a report with someone in room 503; (b) at the bank; (c) eating lunch at a nearby restaurant; (d) practicing a presentation in the conference room; (e) waiting for the section chief in the next room.

2. You are speaking to Yamamoto-san, your company's client. Answer his question based on the following information: This week you are free on Wednesday and Thursday. Next week you are free on Tuesday and Friday.

3. Answer Murata-san's questions based on the following information: (a) you've already eaten lunch; (b) you've already consulted with the section manager; (c) you've already asked Mizuno-sensei; (d) you've already bought a new one.

4. Respond to what an office associate says based on the following information: (a) you are still studying Japanese; (b) Murata-san is still consulting with someone in the conference room; (c) Smith-san is still somewhere in Japan.

5. An aikido club meeting has ended and you were getting ready to leave when a close friend showed up. Yuya, a mutual friend, has already left.

6. Your office associate asks you about Smith-san, who has become an English teacher and is now teaching English somewhere in Japan.

7. Your office associate asks you where Yoshida-san's car is. It's the grey one to the right of the blue one over there.

8. You are looking at two items in a store with an office associate. The item on the right is more expensive than the one on the left.

9. Your office associate asks if you know Taneda-san. You have no idea who Taneda-san is.

Now it's your turn to start the conversation based on the given context. Listen to how the other person reacts to you. For some items, you may not get a verbal response. Don't be concerned if you hear things you have not yet learned.

10. You are about to leave campus with a friend when you realize you left your notebook in the library. Ask your friend to wait while you go get your notebook.

11. Ask an office associate what he will be doing this weekend.

12. You have something difficult to talk about with your *senpai* at work.

13. You are from Ogaki Shokai, meeting someone who regularly works with your company for the first time. (In the sample response, Sasha Morris's name will be used.)

14. Inform an office associate that (a) no one has arrived yet; (b) you haven't consulted with anyone yet; (c) you haven't reported to the section manager yet; (c) you haven't done anything yet.

15. You are introducing yourself to a group of employees at a company where you just started working. Tell them where you are from. (In the sample response, Alberta, a province in Canada, will be used as the location.)

16. An office associate has just asked where you are from. Tell him where you are from. (In the sample response, Oregon will be used as the location.)

17. You are a new employee and have been asked to introduce yourself to the office staff and other employees. Base your self-introduction on the following information: You are from England; you studied abroad in Japan for 8 weeks last year; you arrived in Japan 1 week ago; your hobby is golf. The model will use the name Thomas Hunt, but you should use your own name in your introduction.

18. You and an office associate need to get ready for a meeting with a client at 3:30. Inform your office associate that it's already 3:00, but you haven't done anything yet.
19. You are talking about having a meeting with some other office workers. Ask if it's all right to start at 2:00 p.m.
20. You are taking a photo of a group. Tell the tall person in the yellow T-shirt to move a little more towards the back.
21. A friend is looking at plane tickets and discovers that they are more expensive than the last time she looked. She is now thinking of waiting to buy a ticket. Tell her that it will get (even) more expensive.
22. You have a meeting with your company's client. You have just arrived at the meeting, but you are about a minute late.
23. Ask your section manager if he is busy tomorrow.
24. You have just finished a meeting and are planning on having another meeting tomorrow. Ask the group if it's all right if it's the same time as today's.
25. You have just learned that Yagi-bucho is an excellent tennis player. You are not surprised that someone as accomplished as Yagi-bucho would be great at tennis.

読んでみよう Contextualized reading

Read the information and answer in English the questions that follow.

1. A poster found at a community center.

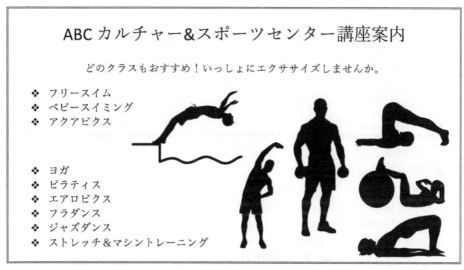

ABC カルチャー＆スポーツセンター講座案内

どのクラスもおすすめ！いっしょにエクササイズしませんか。

- ❖ フリースイム
- ❖ ベビースイミング
- ❖ アクアビクス

- ❖ ヨガ
- ❖ ピラティス
- ❖ エアロビクス
- ❖ フラダンス
- ❖ ジャズダンス
- ❖ ストレッチ＆マシントレーニング

a. What catch phrase is used to attract people?
b. List the courses that use a pool.
c. What types of exercise courses are provided? List all of them.

いつもお世話になっております。

2. A menu from a café.

オーシャンビュー・カフェ

メニュー

お飲み物		お食事	
コーヒー（ホット、アイス）	¥400	ハンバーガー	¥550
エスプレッソ	¥450	ハムサンド	¥650
カプチーノ	¥550	ベジタブルサンド	¥650
ウインナーコーヒー	¥650	パスタ	
ココア	¥350	ミートソース	¥800
		カルボナーラ	¥850
スープ＆サラダ			
トマトスープ	¥500	**デザート**	
オニオンスープ	¥550	アイスクリーム	¥450
グリーンサラダ	¥600	バニラ	
シーザーサラダ	¥650	ストロベリー	
シーフードサラダ	¥700	チョコレート	
		バナナクリームパイ	¥450

a. What is the name of the café?
b. How much does espresso cost?
c. What kind of soups are available?
d. Which salad is the most expensive?
e. What is the most expensive item on the menu?
f. You are a vegetarian. What choices do you have besides soup and salad, drinks, and desserts?
g. What ice cream flavors are available?

いつもお世話になっております。

書き取り Dictation

Listen to the self-introductions at a student gathering and write down in katakana the name of the person, the US state that person comes from, and what the person likes.

	Name	U.S. state	What the person likes
1.			
2.			
3.			
4.			
5.			
6.			

書いてみよう Contextualized writing

Compose a note according to the directions.

1. You are leaving a schedule for part-time workers at your supervisor's office. Attach a sticky note to the envelope for your supervisor, indicating that the schedule is inside. Start by saying that Smith-san hasn't checked (the schedule) yet.

2. You want to get rid of an old computer in your office. Attach a sticky note to it asking your assistant to recycle this computer because it is no longer (already not) working.

Act6

いつもお世話になっております。

3. Your fellow part-time worker, Katherine, asked about a restaurant you went to last week. Attach a sticky note to a menu from the restaurant, telling her that it's the menu from that restaurant (you both know), and tell her that the all of the pasta items here are extremely good.

知ってる? What do you know?

Select the most appropriate option and write the letter in the space on your answer sheet.

1. You tell the new intern that you'll be waiting for her in the lobby tomorrow when she arrives.
   あしたロビーで_____。(BTS 1)

   a. 待っています
   b. 待ちます
   c. 待ちましょう

2. You've been asked what university you'll be going to next year. You reply:
   来年福沢大学に_____。(BTS 1)

   a. 行っています
   b. 行きます
   c. 行きましょう

3. You've been asked what you were doing last night from about 8–10 p.m. You reply:

留学センターで勉強_____。(BTS 1)

a. しています
b. していました
c. しました

4. You tell your classmate that you've been attending Sakamoto-sensei's seminar since last month.

先月から坂本先生のセミナーに_____。(BTS 1)

a. 出ます
b. 出ていました
c. 出ています

5. You tell your roommate that the cookies are done.

クッキーは_____。(BTS 1)

a. できています
b. できます
c. できていました

6. You tell your classmate that you haven't done the homework yet.

宿題はまだ_____。(BTS 3)

a. しなかった
b. していない
c. していなかった

7. You've been asked if you still jog every day. You reply:

ジョギングは_____。(BTS 2, 3)

a. もうしています
b. まだしません
c. もうしていません

8. You're surprised that it's already 2:00. (BTS 2, 3)

a. もう2時です。
b. まだ2時です。
c. もう2時じゃないです。

9. You want to know if it's okay to start from page 25.

２５ページ_____いいですか。(BTS 5)

a. で
b. から
c. からで

10. You're meeting the mayor of the town and formally introducing yourself. You say:

    Your NAME と_____。(BTS 6)

    a. いいます
    b. 申します
    c. おっしゃいます

11. Which of the following can indicate both naming and counting? (BTS 9)

    a. 3時
    b. 3年
    c. 3週間

12. You encourage your guest to drink some more tea.

    お茶_____飲んでください。(BTS 12)

    a. も
    b. もう
    c. もっと

13. You ask for one more of those desserts.

    それ、_____一個ください。(BTS 12)

    a. も
    b. もう
    c. もっと

14. おります is the humble form of _____. (BTS 15)

    a. います
    b. します
    c. 言います

15. You've been asked if you spoke with the new section chief about an important matter.

    You reply, politely: はい、お話_____。(BTS 15)

    a. 申しました
    b. いたしました
    c. おりました

16. You will often hear ~ まして instead of the ~て form when _____. (BTS 16)

    a. requesting a favor of someone
    b. asking a superior a question
    c. making a public announcement

17. You ask your office mate if she went anywhere over the weekend.

    どこ_____行きましたか。(BTS 18, 22)

いつもお世話になっております。

a. にも
b. へは
c. かへ

18. You're wondering if there are any good bookstores around here.

どこ＿＿＿＿＿＿＿＿いい本屋、ありますか。(BTS 18)

a. に
b. か
c. で

19. By using んです in a question, you're＿＿＿＿ a situation. (BTS 19)

a. expressing your doubt about
b. seeking an explanation of
c. offering a solution for

20. In statements, んです is often used to express＿＿＿＿＿＿＿. (BTS 19)

a. agreement
b. reason
c. doubt

21. When you add たい to the stem of a verb, the form that results is ＿＿＿＿. (BTS 20)

a. an adjective
b. a noun
c. a verb

22. Which of the following does not have a たい form? (BTS 20)

a. います
b. します
c. あります

23. You politely offer to make a new poster for your section chief who seems busy with other projects. 私が＿＿＿＿＿＿＿＿＿＿か。(BTS 21)

a. お作りしません
b. お作りしたいんです
c. お作りしましょう

24. You notice that something is different about the design of the new app.

古いの＿＿＿＿＿ちょっと違う。(BTS 25)

a. に
b. と
c. も

25. You're wondering if you should report the news to someone like your junior colleague or the section head. 課長_____後輩に報告しましょうか。(BTS 23)

    a. が
    b. か
    c. と

26. Which of the following does not occur in an affirmative sentence? (BTS 22)

    a. だれも
    b. どれも
    c. どちらも

27. You comment that many exchange students came to the performance.
留学生が_____も来ましたね。(BTS 22)

    a. だれ
    b. 何人
    c. いくら

28. When making a comparison of two options, the noun you use as a reference is followed by _____. (BTS 24)

    a. から
    b. より
    c. と

29. You ask your professor politely if she knows the name of the new school president.
新しい学長の名前を_____か。(BTS 27)

    a. 存じています
    b. 知ります
    c. ご存知です

30. In katakana, the /th/ of *leather* becomes _____. (BTL 3)

    a. /s/
    b. /z/
    c. /j/

31. Which of the following symbols is rarely used in modern Japanese? _____. (BTL 6)

    a. ヲ
    b. オ
    c. フ

いつもお世話になっております。

Appendix A: <ruby>文字練習<rt>もじれんしゅう</rt></ruby> Symbol practice

ひらがな **Hiragana**

Instruction

For each symbol, study the overall shape (top left) and stroke order, then complete every box to the right of it.

Act 2

#1 　一　十　あ
あ　あ
あ

#2 　丶　こ
こ　こ
こ

#3 　そ
そ　そ
そ

#4 | れ

れ れ

れ

#5 丶 と

と と

と

#6 つ カ か

か か

か

#7 ー す

す す

す

#8 ー ナ た た

た た

た

#9 て

て て

て

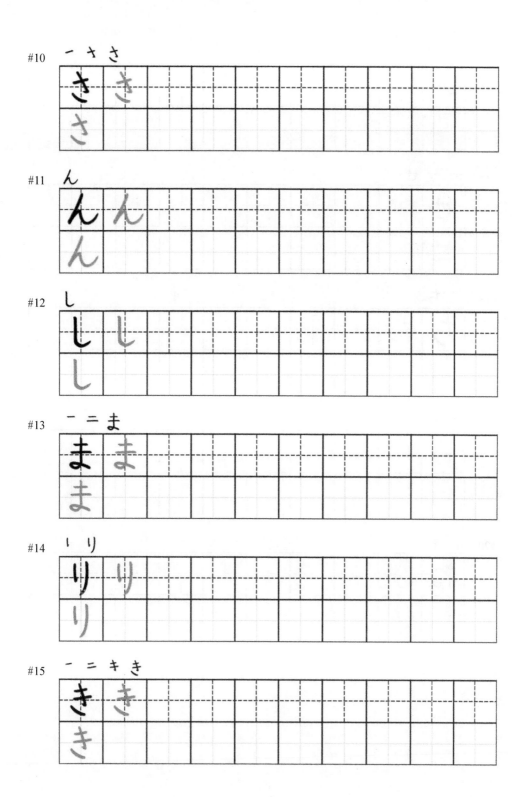

#10 　ー　ナ　さ

#11 　ん

#12 　し

#13 　ー　ニ　ま

#14 　ゝ　り

#15 　ー　ニ　キ　き

#16　い　い

い　い

い

#17　一　ナ　せ

せ　せ

せ

#18　一　ち

ち　ち

ち

#19　、　ら

ら　ら

ら

#20　丨　ね

ね　ね

ね

#21

#22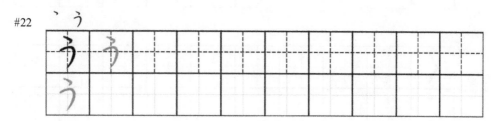

#23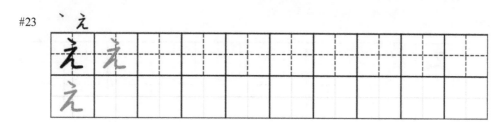

#24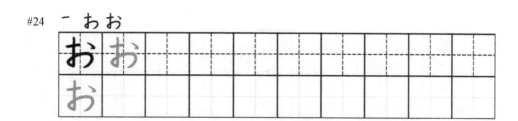

Act 3

#25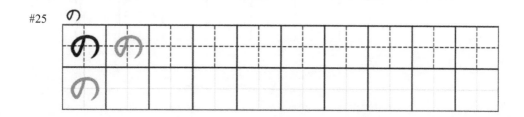

#26 一 ナ 九 な

な な

な

#27 く

く く

く

#28 み み

み み

み

#29 ろ

ろ ろ

ろ

#30 し も も

も も

も

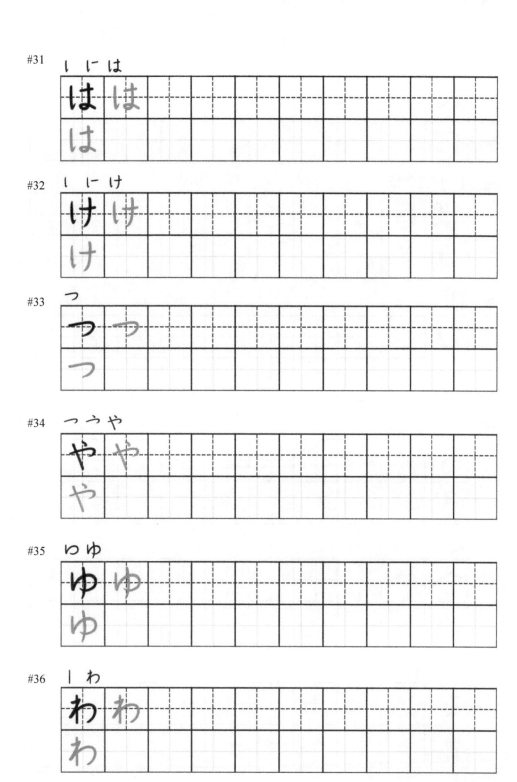

#31　ｌ　ｌに　は
は　は

は

#32　ｌ　ｌに　け
け　け

け

#33　つ
つ　つ

つ

#34　つ　う　や
や　や

や

#35　い　ゆ
ゆ　ゆ

ゆ

#36　ｌ　わ
わ　わ

わ

#37　　い　に　に

に　に
に

#38　　い　に　に　ほ

ほ　ほ
ほ

#39　　ひ

ひ　ひ
ひ

#40　　゛　ふ　ふ　ふ

ふ　ふ
ふ

#41　　へ

へ　へ
へ

#42　　ー　む　む

む　む
む

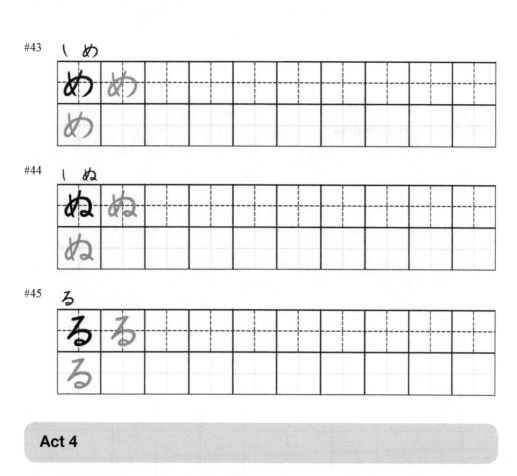

#43　 し　め

#44　し　ぬ

#45　る

Act 4

#46　一　ち　を

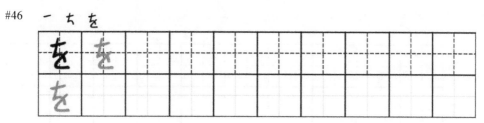

カタカナ **Katakana**

Instruction

For each symbol, study the overall shape (top left) and stroke order, then complete every box to the right of it.

Act 5

#1   フ ア

ア ア

ア

#2   ノ イ

イ イ

イ

#3   ' 'ʼ ウ

ウ ウ

ウ

212

#4 一 丁 エ

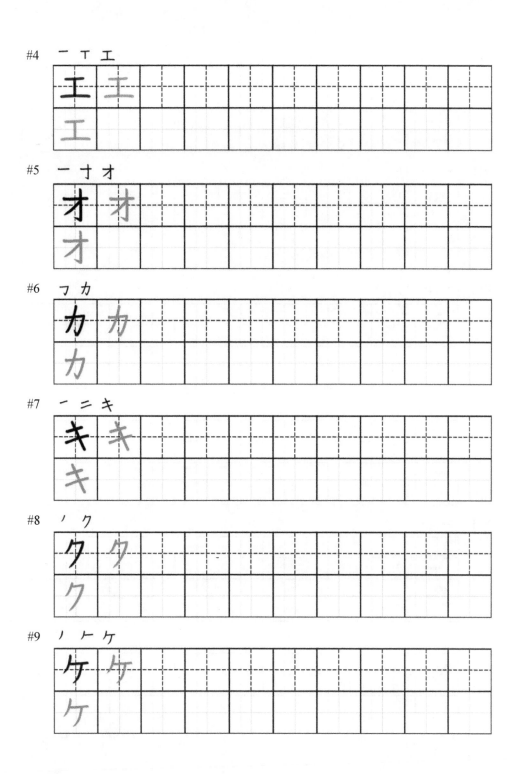

#5 一 オ オ

#6 フ カ

#7 一 二 キ

#8 ノ ク

#9 ノ ト ケ

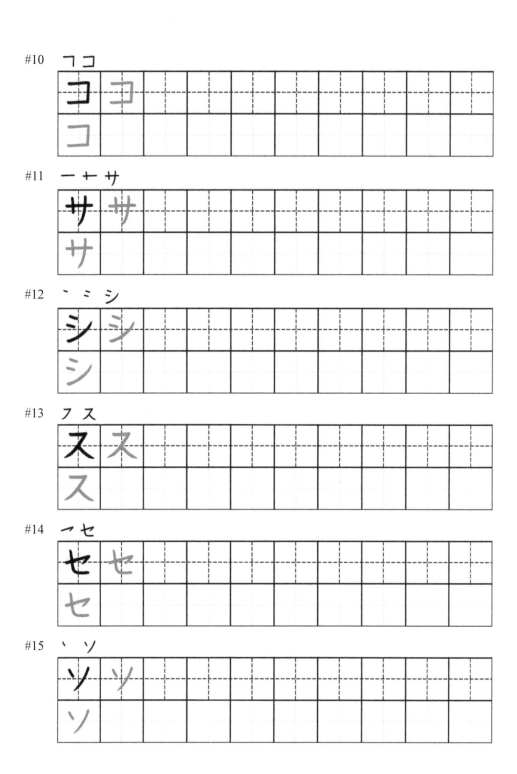

#10 コ

#11 一 十 サ

#12 ン ミ シ

#13 フ ス

#14 ゼ セ

#15 ヽ ソ

#16 ノ ク タ

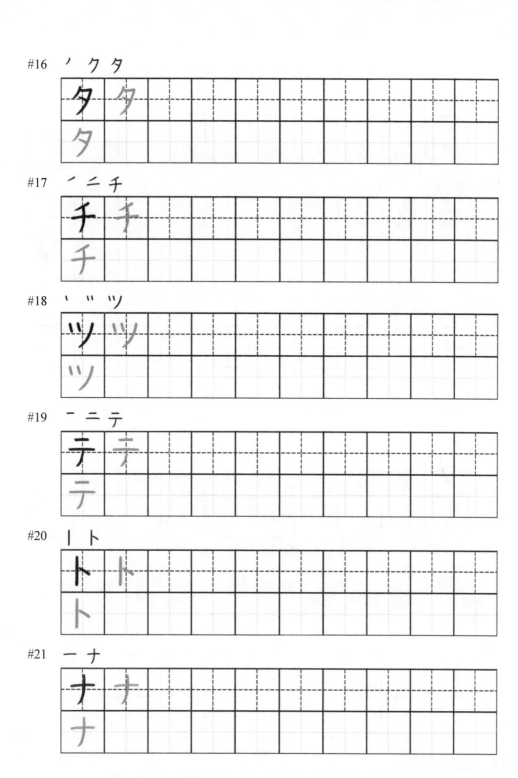

#17 ノ ニ チ

#18 丶 ゛ ツ

#19 ー ニ テ

#20 丨 卜

#21 ー ナ

#22 一 二

#23 フ ヌ

#24 ` ラ ネ ネ

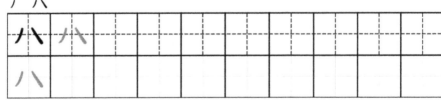

#25 ノ

Act 6

#26 ノ 八

#27 ー ヒ

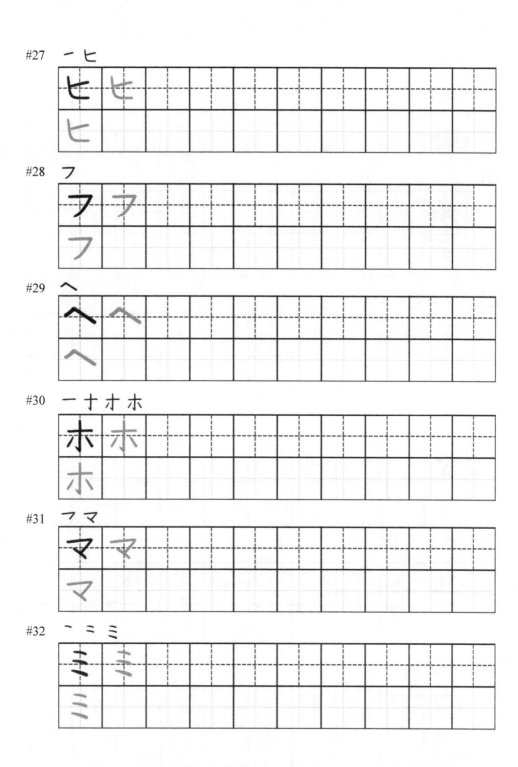

#28 フ

#29 ヘ

#30 ー ナ オ ホ

#31 フ マ

#32 ` ` ミ ミ

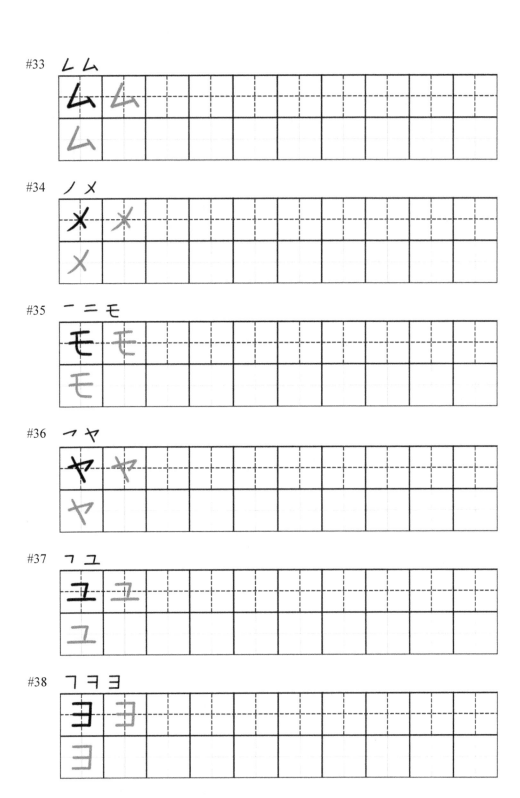

#33 ㄴ ㅿ

#34 ノ メ

#35 ー 二 モ

#36 ⁊ ヤ

#37 フ ユ

#38 フ ヲ ヨ

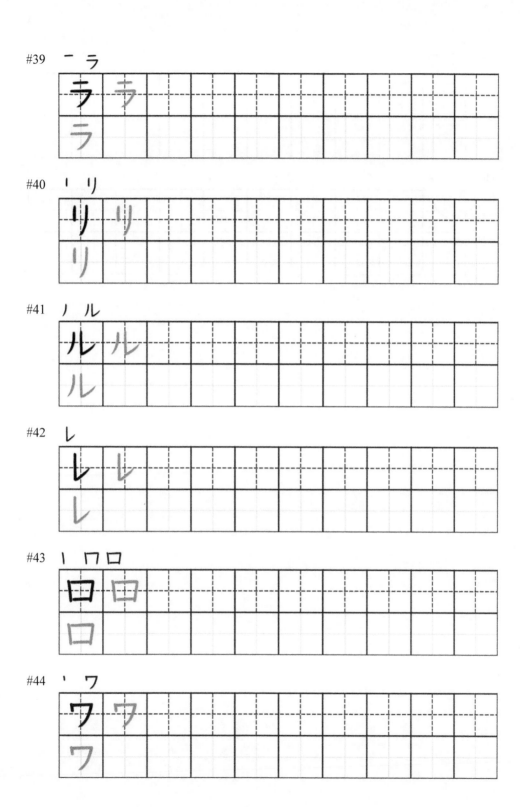

#39 　ー　ラ

#40 　丶　リ

#41 　ノ　ル

#42 　レ

#43 　丨　冂　口

#44 　丶　ワ

#45　フ ヲ

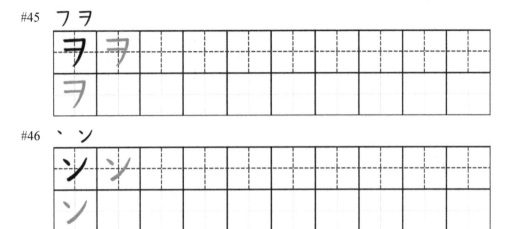

#46　ヽ ソ

Appendix B: Assessment answer sheets

聞いてみよう Listening comprehension

Write your answers to the Listening comprehension questions.

ACT # _____   Date: _____   Name: _____

No.	Q	Your answer
1	a	

221

読んでみよう Contextualized reading

Write your answers to the Contextualized reading questions.

ACT # _____   Date: _____   Name: _____

No.	Q	Your answer
1	a	

書き取り Dictation

Write what you hear.

ACT # _____ Date: _____ Name: _____

No.	Your answer
1	

書<ruby>か<rt>か</rt></ruby>いてみよう Contextualized writing

Write your responses to the Contextualized writing items.

ACT # _____   Date: _____   Name: _____

知ってる? What do you know?

Write your answers to the What do you know? questions.

ACT # _____   Date: _____   Name: _____

1		11		21	
2		12		22	
3		13		23	
4		14		24	
5		15		25	
6		16		26	
7		17		27	
8		18		28	
9		19		29	
10		20		30	

Appendix B

Appendix C: 形 にスポットライト！
Katachi ni supotto-raito! Spotlight on form!
Act 2: negative -*nai desu* forms

Here is a table of all the verbs you have learned so far with -*masu* forms and some -*nai desu* forms. Using romanization, fill in the rest of the blanks with the forms that complete the table. Do you see any irregular forms? As you learn the appropriate hiragana and kanji, you can add the forms in hiragana (furigana) and kanji as well.

-*masu* forms	English	-*nai* forms	English
します *shi-masu*	do	*shi-nai desu*	doesn't do
食べます *tabe-masu*	eat	*tabe-nai desu*	doesn't eat
できます *deki-masu*	can do	*deki-_____*	_____
始めます *hajime-masu*	begin	*hajime-_____*	_____
来ます *ki-masu*	come	*ko-_____*	_____
います *i-masu*	be, exist (animate)	*i-_____*	_____
わかります *wakar-imasu*	understand	*wakar-anai desu*	_____
頑張ります *ganbar-imasu*	do one's best	*ganbar-_____*	_____
終わります *owar-imasu*	end something	*owar-_____*	_____
あります *ar-imasu*	exist (inanimate)	_____	_____
書きます *kak-imasu*	write	*kak-_____*	_____
飲みます *nom-imasu*	drink	*nom-_____*	_____
いただきます *itadak-imasu*	eat; receive (humble)	*itadak-_____*	_____
読みます *yom-imasu*	read	*yom-_____*	_____
行きます *ik-imasu*	go	*ik-_____*	_____

Here is a table of all the adjectives you have learned so far with *-i desu* forms and some *-ku nai desu* forms. Using romanization, fill in the rest of the blanks with the forms that complete the table. Do you see any irregular forms? As you learn the appropriate hiragana and kanji, you can add the forms in hiragana (furigana) and kanji as well.

-i *desu* forms	English	*-ku nai* forms	English
すごいです *sugoi desu*	amazing	*sugoku nai desu*	it's not amazing
いいです *ii desu*	good	*yoku nai desu*	it's not good
よろしいです *yoroshii desu*	good (polite)	_____	it's not good
おいしいです *oishii desu*	delicious	_____	_____
おもしろいです *omoshiroi desu*	interesting/funny	_____	_____
忙しいです *isogashii desu*	busy	_____	_____
高いです *takai desu*	expensive	_____	_____
安いです *yasui desu*	cheap	_____	_____
大きいです *ookii desu*	big	_____	_____
小さいです *chiisai desu*	small	_____	_____
遠いです *tooi desu*	far	_____	_____
近いです *chikai desu*	close by	_____	_____
易しいです *yasashii desu*	easy	_____	_____
難しいです *muzukashii desu*	difficult	_____	_____

Here is a table of many nouns you have learned so far with *desu* forms and some *-ja nai desu* forms. Using romanization, fill in the rest of the blanks with the forms that complete the table. As you learn the appropriate hiragana and kanji, you can add the forms in hiragana (furigana) and kanji as well.

Noun *desu* forms	English	Noun *ja nai desu* forms	English
これです *kore desu*	it's this	*kore ja nai desu*	it's not this
大丈夫です *daijoobu desu*	it's fine	*daijoobu ja nai desu*	it's not fine
平気です *heiki desu*	it's all right	_____	it's not all right
あしたです *ashita desu*	it's tomorrow	_____	_____
携帯です *keitai desu*	it's a cell phone	_____	_____
テストです *tesuto desu*	it's a test	_____	_____
好きです *suki desu*	it's pleasant	_____	_____
朝ごはんです *asa-gohan desu*	it's breakfast	_____	_____
焼き鳥です *yakitori desu*	it's *yakitori*	_____	_____
そちらです *sochira desu*	it's there	_____	_____
寮です *ryoo desu*	it's a dorm	_____	_____
そうです *soo desu*	it's like that	_____	_____
駅です *eki desu*	it's the station	_____	_____
学校です *gakkoo desu*	it's a school	_____	_____

Appendix D: 形<ruby>かたち</ruby>にスポットライト！ *Katachi ni supotto-raito! Spotlight on form! Act 3: -mashoo forms; Noun -ja nai forms*

Here is a table of all the verbs you have learned so far with *-masu* forms and some *-mashoo* forms. Using Romanization, fill in the rest of the blanks with the forms that complete the table. Do you see any irregular forms? As you learn the appropriate hiragana and kanji, you can add the forms in hiragana (furigana) and kanji as well.

-masu forms	English	*-mashoo* forms	English
勉強します *benkyoo-shi-masu*	study	*benkyoo-shi-mashoo*	let's study
食べます *tabe-masu*	eat	*tabe-mashoo*	let's eat
見ます *mi-masu*	look at	*mi-_____*	let's have a look
始めます *hajime-masu*	begin	*hajime-_____*	_____
来ます *ki-masu*	come	*ki-_____*	_____
います *i-masu*	be, exist (animate)	*i-_____*	_____
帰ります *kaer-imasu*	return; go home	*kaer-imashoo*	_____
終わります *owar-imasu*	end something	*owar-_____*	_____
待ちます *mach-imasu*	wait	*mach-_____*	_____
書きます *kak-imasu*	write	*kak-_____*	_____
飲みます *nom-imasu*	drink	*nom-_____*	_____
話します *hanash-imasu*	talk	*hanash-_____*	_____
会います *a-imasu*	meet	*a-_____*	_____

Here is a table of many nouns that come up in this Act with *desu* forms and some negative *-ja nai desu* forms. Using romanization, fill in the rest of the blanks with the forms that complete the table. As you learn the appropriate hiragana and kanji, you can add the forms in hiragana (furigana) and kanji as well.

Noun *desu* forms	English	*Noun ja nai desu* forms	English
これです *kore desu*	it's this	*kore ja nai desu*	it's not this
病気です *byooki desu*	she's sick	*byooki ja nai desu*	she's not sick
アプリです *apuri desu*	it's an app	_____	it's not an app
つぎです *tsugi desu*	it's next	_____	_____
だめです *dame desu*	it's bad, not good	_____	_____
図書館です *toshokan desu*	it's a library	_____	_____
友達です *tomodachi desu*	he's a friend	_____	_____
同僚です *dooryoo desu*	she's a colleague	_____	_____
雨です *ame desu*	it's raining	_____	_____
同じです *onaji desu*	it's the same	_____	_____

Appendix E: 形<ruby>かたち</ruby>にスポットライト！ *Katachi ni supotto-raito!* Spotlight on form! Act 4: Negative *-nakatta* desu and Noun + *datta* forms

Here is a table of verbs that come up in this Act with *-masen deshita* forms and some *-(a) nakatta desu* forms. Using romanization, fill in the rest of the blanks with the forms that complete the table. Are you picking up the patterns for verbs? As you learn the appropriate hiragana and kanji, you can add the forms in hiragana (furigana) and kanji as well.

-masen deshita forms	English	*-(a)nakatta desu* forms
食べませんでした *tabe-masen deshita*	didn't eat	*tabe-nakatta desu*
話しませんでした *hanash-imasen deshita*	didn't talk	*hanas-anakatta desu*
会いませんでした *a-imasen deshita*	didn't meet	*aw-anakatta desu*
取りませんでした *tor-imasen deshita*	didn't take	*tor-_____*
作りませんでした *tsukur-imasen deshita*	didn't make	*tsukur-_____*
考えませんでした *kangae-masen deshita*	didn't think about	*kangae-_____*
聞きませんでした *kik-imasen deshita*	didn't listen	*kik-_____*
乗りませんでした *nor-imasen deshita*	didn't get on board	*nor-_____*
手伝いませんでした *tetsuda-imasen deshita*	didn't help	*tetsudaw-_____*
かかりませんでした *kakar-imasen deshita*	didn't take	*kakar-_____*
使いませんでした *tsuka-imasen deshita*	didn't use	*tsukaw-_____*
頑張りませんでした *ganbar-imasen deshita*	didn't persevere	*ganbar-_____*

Here is a table of many nouns that come up in this Act with *ja arimasen deshita* forms and some *-ja nakatta* forms. Using romanization, fill in the rest of the blanks with the forms that complete the table. As you learn the appropriate hiragana and kanji, you can add the forms in hiragana (furigana) and kanji as well.

Noun *ja arimasen deshita* forms	English	Noun *ja nakatta* forms
専門じゃありませんでした *senmon ja arimasen deshita*	it wasn't a specialization	*kore ja nakatta desu*
２時間じゃありませんでした *ni-jikan ja arimasen deshita*	it wasn't two hours	*ni-jikan ja nakatta desu*
工学じゃありませんでした *koogaku ja arimasen deshita*	it wasn't engineering	_____
言語学じゃありませんでした *gengogaku ja arimasen deshita*	it wasn't linguistics	_____
大変じゃありませんでした *taihen ja arimasen deshita*	it wasn't terrible	_____
おとといじゃありませんでした *ototoi ja arimasen deshita*	it wasn't the day before yesterday	_____
教室じゃありませんでした *kyooshitsu ja arimasen deshita*	it wasn't a classroom	_____
公園じゃありませんでした *kooen ja arimasen deshita*	it wasn't a park	_____
今年じゃありませんでした *kotoshi ja arimasen deshita*	it wasn't this year	_____
明治じゃありませんでした *Meiji ja arimasen deshita*	it wasn't the Meiji Era	_____
さっきじゃありませんでした *sakki ja arimasen deshita*	it wasn't a while ago	_____
自転車じゃありませんでした *jitensha ja arimasen deshita*	it wasn't a bicycle	_____
土曜日じゃありませんでした *doyoobi ja arimasen deshita*	it wasn't Saturday	_____

Here is a table of adjectives that come up in the last two Acts with *-ku arimasen deshita* forms and some *-ku nakatta* forms. Using romanization, fill in the rest of the blanks with the forms that complete the table. As you learn the appropriate hiragana and kanji, you can add the forms in hiragana (furigana) and kanji as well.

-ku arimasen deshita forms	English	*ku nakatta* forms
<ruby>新<rt>あたら</rt></ruby>しくありませんでした *atarashiku arimasen deshita*	it wasn't new	*atarashiku nakatta desu*
<ruby>古<rt>ふる</rt></ruby>くありませんでした *furuku arimasen deshita*	it wasn't old	*furuku nakatta desu*
<ruby>使<rt>つか</rt></ruby>いやすくありませんでした *tsukaiyasuku arimasen deshita*	it wasn't easy to use	_____
<ruby>使<rt>つか</rt></ruby>いにくくありませんでした *tsukainikuku arimasen deshita*	it wasn't hard to use	_____
<ruby>青<rt>あお</rt></ruby>くありませんでした *aoku arimasen deshita*	it wasn't blue	_____
<ruby>黒<rt>くろ</rt></ruby>くありませんでした *kuroku arimasen deshita*	it wasn't black	_____
かわいくありませんでした *kawaiku arimasen deshita*	it wasn't cute	_____
<ruby>早<rt>はや</rt></ruby>くありませんでした *hayaku arimasen deshita*	they weren't early	_____
<ruby>遅<rt>おそ</rt></ruby>くありませんでした *osoku arimasen deshita*	she wasn't late	_____
<ruby>白<rt>しろ</rt></ruby>くありませんでした *shiroku arimasen deshita*	it wasn't white	_____

Here is a table of many nouns that come up in this Act with *da* forms (remember that *rekishi da* 'it's history' is a bit blunter than *rekishi* 'it's history' without *da*) and some *-datta* forms. Using romanization, fill in the rest of the blanks with the forms that complete the table. As you learn the appropriate hiragana and kanji, you can add the forms in hiragana (furigana) and kanji as well.

Noun *da* forms	English	Noun *datta* forms	English
歴史(だ) rekishi (da)	it's history	*rekishi datta*	it was history
２時間(だ) ni-jikan (da)	it's two hours	*ni-jikan datta*	it was two hours
工学(だ) koogaku (da)	it's engineering	_____	it was engineering
専攻(だ) senkoo (da)	it's my major	_____	_____
大変(だ) taihen (da)	it's terrible	_____	_____
去年(だ) kyonen (da)	it's last year	_____	_____
教室(だ) kyooshitsu (da)	it's a classroom	_____	_____
公園(だ) kooen (da)	it's a park	_____	_____
本当(だ) hontoo (da)	it's true	_____	_____
昭和(だ) Shoowa (da)	it's the Showa Era	_____	_____
さっき(だ) sakki (da)	it's a while ago	_____	_____
自転車(だ) jitensha (da)	it's a bicycle	_____	_____
月曜日(だ) getsuyoobi (da)	it's Monday	_____	_____

Appendix F: 形<ruby>かたち</ruby>にスポットライト！
Spotlight on form! Act 5: 〜て forms

Here is a table of all of the verbs you have learned so far with their 〜ない forms and 〜て forms. Fill in the rest of the blanks with the forms that complete the table. Are you picking up the patterns for verbs? This time, you should use hiragana for completing the table. When the verb is typically written in kanji, the character is provided to get you started. Be careful of おくりがな.

ます forms	English	〜ない forms	〜て forms
決<ruby>き</ruby>めます kime-masu	decide	決<ruby>き</ruby>めない kime-nai	決<ruby>き</ruby>めて kime-te
見<ruby>み</ruby>ます mi-masu	see	見<ruby>み</ruby>ない mi-nai	見<ruby>み</ruby>て mi-te
食<ruby>た</ruby>べます tabe-masu	eat	食<ruby>た</ruby>べない tabe-nai	食<ruby>た</ruby>べて tabe-te
できます deki-masu	can do	でき＿＿＿＿＿	でき＿＿＿＿＿
います i-masu	be, exist (animate)	い＿＿＿＿＿	い＿＿＿＿＿
始<ruby>はじ</ruby>めます hajime-masu	begin something	始<ruby>はじ</ruby>め＿＿＿＿＿	始<ruby>はじ</ruby>め＿＿＿＿＿
考<ruby>かんが</ruby>えます kangae-masu	think	考<ruby>かんが</ruby>え＿＿＿＿＿	考<ruby>かんが</ruby>え＿＿＿＿＿
借<ruby>か</ruby>ります kari-masu	borrow (5-3)	借<ruby>か</ruby>り＿＿＿＿＿	借<ruby>か</ruby>り＿＿＿＿＿
教<ruby>おし</ruby>えます oshie-masu	teach (5-5)	教<ruby>おし</ruby>え＿＿＿＿＿	教<ruby>おし</ruby>え＿＿＿＿＿

ます forms	English	〜ない forms	〜て forms
わかります wakar-imasu	understand	わからない wakar-anai	わかって wakat-te
頑張<ruby>がんば</ruby>ります ganbar-imasu	do one's best	頑張<ruby>がんば</ruby>＿＿＿＿＿	頑張<ruby>がんば</ruby>＿＿＿＿＿
終<ruby>お</ruby>わります owar-imasu	end something	終<ruby>お</ruby>わ＿＿＿＿＿	終<ruby>お</ruby>わ＿＿＿＿＿
取<ruby>と</ruby>ります tor-imasu	take	取<ruby>と</ruby>＿＿＿＿＿	取<ruby>と</ruby>＿＿＿＿＿
あります ar-imasu	exist (inanimate)	ない nai	あ＿＿＿＿＿
作<ruby>つく</ruby>ります tsukur-imasu	make	作<ruby>つく</ruby>＿＿＿＿＿	作<ruby>つく</ruby>＿＿＿＿＿
帰<ruby>かえ</ruby>ります kaer-imasu	return	帰<ruby>かえ</ruby>＿＿＿＿＿	帰<ruby>かえ</ruby>＿＿＿＿＿
乗<ruby>の</ruby>ります nor-imasu	ride, get onboard	乗<ruby>の</ruby>＿＿＿＿＿	乗<ruby>の</ruby>＿＿＿＿＿

ます forms	English	～ない forms	～て forms
かかります *kakar-imasu*	take (time/money)	かか＿＿＿＿＿	かか＿＿＿＿＿
使います *tsuka-imasu*	use	使わない *tsukaw-anai*	使って *tsukat-te*
言います *i-imasu*	is called, say	言＿＿＿＿＿	言＿＿＿＿＿
会います *a-imasu*	see, meet	会＿＿＿＿＿	会＿＿＿＿＿
違います *chiga-imasu*	different from	違＿＿＿＿＿	違＿＿＿＿＿
買います *ka-imasu*	buy	買＿＿＿＿＿	買＿＿＿＿＿
手伝います *tetsuda-imasu*	help	手伝＿＿＿＿＿	手伝＿＿＿＿＿
構います *kama-imasu*	mind, care	構＿＿＿＿＿	構＿＿＿＿＿
待ちます *mach-imasu*	wait	待たない *mat-anai*	待って *mat-te*
飲みます *nom-imasu*	drink	飲まない *nom-anai*	飲んで *non-de*
読みます *yom-imasu*	read	読＿＿＿＿＿	読＿＿＿＿＿
死にます *shin-imasu*	die	死なない *shin-anai*	死んで *shin-de*
呼びます *yob-imasu*	call	呼ばない *yob-anai*	呼んで *yon-de*
話します *hanash-imasu*	talk	話さない *hanas-anai*	話して *hanashi-te*
書きます *kak-imasu*	write	書かない *kak-anai*	書いて *kai-te*
いただきます *itadak-imasu*	eat; receive (humble)	いただ＿＿＿＿＿	いただ＿＿＿＿＿
聞きます *kik-imasu*	hear; listen	聞＿＿＿＿＿	聞＿＿＿＿＿
行きます *ik-imasu*	go	行＿＿＿＿＿	行って *it-te*
急ぎます *isog-imasu*	hurry	急がない *isog-anai*	急いで *isoi-de*

ます forms	English	～ない forms	～て forms
来ます *ki-masu*	come	こない *ko-nai*	きて *ki-te*
します *shi-masu*	do	しない *shi-nai*	して *shi-te*
勉強します	study	勉強＿＿＿＿＿	勉強＿＿＿＿＿
仕事します	work	仕事＿＿＿＿＿	仕事＿＿＿＿＿
宿題します	do homework	宿題＿＿＿＿＿	宿題＿＿＿＿＿
授業します	conduct a class	授業＿＿＿＿＿	授業＿＿＿＿＿
会議します	hold a meeting	会議＿＿＿＿＿	会議＿＿＿＿＿

Appendix G: Answer keys

0-1C What should you do?
1. d; 2. a; 3. e; 4. c; 5. d; 6. b; 7. f; 8. a; 9. c; 10. h; 11. e; 12. g; 13. c; 14. b; 15. f; 16. a; 17. d; 18. i; 19. d; 20. g

0-2C What should you do?
3. e; 4. j; 5. a; 6. j; 7. f; 8. h; 9. c; 10. b; 11. d; 12. g; 13. i; 14 b. ;15. j; 16. a; 17. l; 18. f; 19. j; 20. e

0-3C Mora count
Group 3. c; Group 4. a; Group 5. c

0-4C Mora count
Group 3. d; Group 4. a; Group 5. d

0-5C Mora count
3. (2); 4. (2); 5. (3); 6. (4); 7. (4); 8. (5); 9. (3); 10. (3); 11. (4); 12. (3); 13. (4); 14. (5); 15. (3)

0-6C Mora count
3. (5); 4. (3); 5. (6); 6. (3); 7. (4); 8. (6); 9. (6); 10. (5); 11. (4); 12. (3); 13. (4); 14. (6); 15. (7)

0-7C Accent
Group 3. a; Group 4. c; Group 5. b

0-8C Accent
3. LHHH; 4. HL; 5. HLLL; 6. LHH; 7. HLLL; 8. HLL; 9. LHHL; 10. HLLL

0-9C Accent
3. HLLLL; 4. LHHHH; 5. LHHHH; 6. LHHHHH; 7. LHHHHL; 8. LHHHHL; 9. LHHLLL; 10. LHHHHHHL

Act 1

1-1-1C Identifying the actors
3. Shirai & Sasha; 4. Brian Wang & Kanda; 5. Sakamoto Ichiro & Morris; 6. Takashi & Yamada Eri

1-1-2P Checking if everybody is here
Ms. Kanda (○); Mr. Shirai (○); Professor Sakamoto (○); Mr. Brian Wang (○); Ms. Sasha Morris (✗); Ms. Yamada (○)

1-2-1C What's going on?
3. a; 4. d; 5. b

1-2-2P What would you say?
3. a; 4. b; 5. a

1-3-1P *Onegai-shimasu*
3. N; 4. Y; 5. N; 6. Y; 7. Y

1-4-1P What would you say?
3. a; 4. b; 5. c

1-5-1C What are they saying?
3. f (Y); 4. g (N); 5. e (N); 6. a (N); 7. c (Y); 8. d (Y)

1-6-1C What's going on?
3. e; 4. b; 5. d; 6. f

1-7-1C Listening for the name
3. Kaoru; 4. Kanda Kenta; 5. Sakamoto Miki; 6. Zhang; 7. Shirai Masao

1-7-2C Finding the one that doesn't belong
3. b; 4. c; 5. c

1-8-1CP Mora count
3. (9); 4. (5); 5. (6); 6. (2); 7. (6); 8. (3); 9. (8); 10. (2); 11. (4); 12. (8)

1-9-1P Mora count
3. (4); 4. (2); 5. (4); 6. (4); 7. (6); 8. (3); 9. (4); 10. (1)

1-9-2P Does that sound right?
3. b; 4. b; 5. d

1-10-1C What's going on?

3. c; 4. b; 5. a; 6. a; 7. a; 8. a; 9. b; 10. c; 11. a; 12. c

1-11-1C What's going on?

3. e; 4. d; 5. c

1-12-1C What's going on?

3. e; 4. c; 5. d

1-14-1P Mora count

3. (3); 4. (7); 5. (5); 6. (6); 7. (9); 8. (8); 9. (5); 10. (7)

1-15-1R Symbol recognition

3. 博; 4. 願; 5. no kanji; 6. 神田; 7. 僕; 一郎; 8. 失礼; 9. 疲; 様; 10. 京都駅; 11. 帰; 12. 先; 13. no kanji

1-15-2R Symbol recognition

3. ドーム; 4. ミーティング; 5. no katakana; 6. ブライアン・ワン; 7. バイバイ; 8. サーシャ・モリス; 9. no katakana; 10. ヤサイクル; 11. ゴミ; 12. エコ

聞いてみよう *Kiite miyoo* Listening comprehension

1. a. they're friends; b. Kenta; 2. a. they're friends; b. they're saying good-bye; 3. a. in the evening after work; b. the man; 4. a. the man; 5. a. they are meeting for the first time; b. Yagi Keiko; c. Shirai; 6. a. their gratitude; b. Amy Chou

知ってる? *Shitte'ru?* What do you know?

1	C	11	C	21	A
2	B	12	B	22	C
3	A	13	C	23	
4	C	14	A	24	
5	B	15	B	25	
6	A	16	C	26	
7	C	17	C	27	
8	C	18	A	28	
9	B	19	B	29	
10	C	20	A	30	

2-0-1C Responding to instructional expressions

3. b; 4. e; 5. g; 6. f; 7. a; 8. d; 9. h; 10. b; 11. d; 12. f; 13. c; 14 g. ;15. a; 16. c; 17. e; 18. b; 19. g; 20. h

2-0-2C Responding appropriately

3. d; 4. b; 5. a; 6. c; 7. b; 8. a; 9. d

2-0-3C What's going on?

3. a; 4. f; 5. g; 6. e; 7. b

2-1-1C Yes or no?

3. b; 4. a; 5. b; 6. a; 7. a; 8. b; 9. a; 10. a

2-2-1C Checking the schedule

today: homework, test, meeting, work; tomorrow: call

2-2-2C Knowing where they are coming from

3. a; 4. c; 5. b; 6. a; 7. b; 8. a; 9. c; 10. a; 11. b; 12. a

2-3-1C What's being offered?

3. a; 4. g; 5. m; 6. c; 7. f; 8. j; 9. k; 10. i; 11. h

2-3-2C Accepted or declined?

3. a; 4. a; 5. a; 6. a; 7. a; 8. d; 9. d; 10. a

2-3-3CP Inviting a colleague

3. accepted; 4. accepted; 5. accepted; 6. accepted; 7. declined; 8. accepted; 9. accepted

2-5-1C What's going on?

3. c; 4. b; 5. a

2-5-2C Asking or stating

3. Question; 4. Statement; 5. Question; 6. Question; 7. Statement; 8. Statement; 9. Question

2-5-3C Acknowledgment or disbelief? Asking or stating?

3. disbelief; 4. acknowledgment; 5. acknowledgment; 6. disbelief

2-6-1C What's going on?

3. b; 4. a; 5. b; 6. a; 7. b; 8. a; 9. b; 10. b; 11. b

2-6-2C What's the style?

3. b; 4. a; 5. b; 6. a; 7. a; 8. a; 9. b

2-7-1C Where is it?

3. a; 4. b; 5. a; 6. c; 7. c

2-8-1C What's going on?

3. a; 4. b; 5. a

2-9-1R Identifying things and people

3. a; 4. c; 5. d; 6. c; 7. c; 8. a

2-9-2R Asking various questions

3. yes/no; 4. wh; 5. yes/no; 6. yes/no; 7. yes/no; 8. yes/no

2-9-3W Writing furigana

3. かねこ　よしき; 4. すだ　ともえ; 5. ありやま　とうま; 6. ふくち　れい

聞いてみよう *Kiite miyoo* Listening comprehension

1. a. the teacher; b. he is late; 2. a. take out the file; b. she turns down his request; c. for making the request; 3. a. finish working; b. the woman; 4. a. today; b. at home; c. it's fine with him; 5. a. it's interesting; b. it's not particularly interesting; c. no, he doesn't; 6. a. Kanda-san; b. he's in a meeting; c. she's not entirely certain; 7. a. a report; b. he's surprised and concerned; c. she is not concerned; 8. a. he offers to help with something; b. near Mrs. Shirai; c. easy; 9. a. an invitation; b. she turns him down; c. she has a test tomorrow; 10. a. he invites her to have lunch; b. she accepts; c. to go to a *soba* restaurant; d. enthusiastically

読んでみよう *Yonde miyoo* Contextualized reading

Handwritten memos

1. a. to thank you for the folder; 2. a. to thank you for the homemade sweets

Text messages

1. a. Whether I am busy now or not; 2. a. where I am (whether I'm at home); 3. a. Thank you! It looks delicious; b. whether it is expensive or not

書き取り *Kakitori* dictation

1. きれいですね。
2. どちらですか。

3. いただきます。
4. おいしいですよ。
5. これ、しませんか。
6. あれ、ありますか。
7. ごちそうさまでした。
8. ありがとうございました。

書いてみよう *Kaite miyoo* Contextualized writing

1. これ、ありがとうございました。
2. これですか。

知ってる? *Shitte'ru?* What do you know?

1	A	11	B	21	
2	B	12	C	22	
3	C	13	B	23	
4	A	14	A	24	
5	B	15	B	25	
6	B	16	B	26	
7	A	17		27	
8	C	18		28	
9	A	19		29	
10	C	20		30	

Act 3

3-1-1CP Asking about acronyms
3. no good; 4. office lady; 5. commercial message; 6. Japanese Student Organization

3-2-1C What's going on?
3. It's not today; 4. It's not difficult; 5. It is tomorrow; 6. It's not cheap; 7. He can't do it; 8. It's not Shirai-san; 9. It is expensive; 10. It's not medicine; 11. She doesn't understand; 12. He won't begin; 13. Invitation; 14. It is pretty; 15. It is far away; 16. He doesn't have it; 17. Invitation; 18. It's not big; 19. He won't eat.

3-3-1C What's right?
3. It's a papaya. 4. It's a mechanical pencil. 5. The meeting is tomorrow at 9:30. 6. The "J" stands for 'joint.' 7. The person is not Mizuno. 8. It's a *saakuru*.

3-3-2C What's the loanword?
3. ice cream; 4. soccer; 5. Los Angeles; 6. love songs; 7. orange juice

3-4-1C What time is the train?
3. 11:39 a.m.; 4. 1:56 p.m.; 5. 4:35 p.m.; 6. 7:08 p.m.; 7. 8:13 p.m.; 8. 2:24 p.m.; 9. 9:02 a.m.

3-4-2C Where did they study that language?
3. French at Oxford University; 4. French at Waseda University; 5. Spanish at graduate school in Texas (Texas Tech); 6. Korean at Kyoto University (Kyodai stands for Kyoto Daigaku); 7. Chinese at UCLA; 8. English in high school

3-5-1C Getting the details
Conversation 1: 3. delicious meals; 4. far; 5. today and tomorrow; 6. Japanese (language); Conversation 2: 7. ramen; 8. over there (away from both speakers); 9. price (expensive); 10. not "off", *ofu*

3-5-2C How many are there?
3. notebooks (29); 4. pens (63); 5. pens (240); 6. notebooks (73); 7. pencils (450); 8. paper (820)

3-5-4P Doing some quick math
3. pens $20 \times 8 = 160$ and notebooks $150 \times 4 = 600$; total = 760; 4. pens $30 \times 6 = 180$ and notebooks $100 \times 8 = 800$; total = 980; 5. pens $57 \times 5 = 285$ and notebooks $200 \times 3 = 600$; total = 885; 6. pens $33 \times 6 = 198$ and notebooks $270 \times 2 = 540$; total = 738

3-6-1C Identifying owners
umbrella—Takashi Matsuura; ticket—Kanda-san; bag—Mr. Shirai; laptop—Division Chief Yagi; pile of paper—Amy

3-7-1R Asking questions
3. yes/no; 4. wh; 5. yes/no; 6. wh; 7. wh; 8. wh

3-7-2R Inviting someone to do something together
3. d; 4. c; 5. e; 6. a

3-7-3W Nouns modifying nouns
3. な; 4. の; 5. な; 6. の; 7. の; 8. の, な

3-8-2R: X or Y?
3. a; 4. b; 5. g; 6. d; 7. c

3-8-3W Filling in the blanks

3. け(れ)ど; 4. も; 5. け(れ)ど; 6. は; 7. も; も; 8. け(れ)ど

3-9-1R: Let's do X together

3. b; 4. g; 5. d; 6. c; 7. f

3-9-2R Correcting information

3. c; 4. a; 5. b; 6. g; 7. e; 8. f

3-9-3R Uses of では

3. Transition; 4. Transition; 5. Negation; 6. Negation

3-9-4W Using furigana

3. ほった　りゅうた; 4. むかい　めい; 5. なかい　りょうすけ; 6. にくそん・ふるかわ; 7. わだ　ゆきこ; 8. へんりー・ひらた

3-9-5W Using furigana

3. ねぬのかわ; 4. まほむら; 5. べつっぷ; 6. りゆうがちさき; 7. けやき(✓); 8. ぬめぐるろ

聞いてみよう *Kiite miyoo* Listening Comprehension

1. a. the time; b. 3:00; 2. a. his bag, red; b. a college logo; c. Sasha; 3. a. Takeda; b. Aoi Publishing; c. Yamamoto-san; d. today is her day off; 4. a. Jake and Takashi; b. the French teacher; 5. a. if she understands Chinese; b. translate it into Japanese; c. she isn't helpful; 6. a. if he has time next weekend; b. she wants to invite him to play golf; c. not play golf; 7. a. a wallet; b. Takashi; c. ID card

読んでみよう *Yonde miyoo* Contextualized reading

(1)a. everyone to eat the food in the container
(2)a. whether the cell phone (pictured in the attachment) belongs to Shirai-san
(3)a. the time of the meeting tomorrow; b. the meeting is at 4:30 instead of 4:00
(4)a. to do today's homework as a group (everyone) at the library on campus.

書き取り *Kakitori* dictation

1. どうぞ。
2. おはよう。

3. いいですか?
4. おはようございます。
5. こんにちは。
6. こんばんは、
7. どうもすみません。
8. ありがとうございました。
9. いただきます。
10. ごちそうさまでした。
11. どうぞよろしく。
12. おやすみなさい。
13. じゃ、またあとで。

書かいてみよう *Kaite miyoo* Contextualized writing

1. これ(は)、だれのですか。
2. ごちそうさまでした。これ、よかったらみなさんでどうぞ。
3. これ、やっぱりとてもおもしろいですよ。あさってしませんか。
4. さとう　たける;ぬのかわ　りゅうたろう

知しってる? *Shitte'ru?* What do you know?

1	B	11	A	21	A
2	A	12	A	22	A
3	B	13	B	23	A
4	C	14	A	24	B
5	C	15	B	25	B
6	B	16	B	26	C
7	C	17	A	27	A
8	A	18	B	28	C
9	A	19	C	29	B
10	B	20	C	30	

Act 4

4-1-1C Non-past or past?
3. non-past; 4. non-past; 5. past; 6. past; 7. non-past; 8. past; 9. non-past; 10. past; 11. non-past; 12. past

4-2-1C What field of study is mentioned?
3. physics; 4. engineering; 5. religion; 6. linguistics; 7. mathematics; 8. literature

4-2-2C What's being asked?
3. a pen that's not black; 4. a bag that's not black; 5. cake that's smaller; 6. a notebook that's cheaper; 7. a T-shirt that's not white; 8. a book that's not so difficult.

4-3-1C What's being asked?
3. b; 4. a; 5. b; 6. a; 7. b; 8. b; 9. b

4-4-1C What day is it?
3. 3; 4. 27; 5. 5; 6. 16; 7. 6; 8. 8; 9. 20

4-5-1C Waiting for someone
3. who (Nakamura); 4. for whom (Murata); 5. for whom (Suzuki); 6. who (Kanda); 7. for whom (Ikegami)

4-6-1C Naming or counting time?
3. naming (2:50); 4. naming (5:30); 5. counting (one hour); 6. counting (thirty minutes); 7. counting (one hour thirty minutes); 8. naming (14:06); 9. naming (11:20)

4-7-1R Reporting where something or someone was or where something was taking place
3. で; 4. に; 5. で; 6. で; 7. に; 8. で

4-7-2R Expressing or asking about limitation
3. e; 4. b; 5. c; 6. a

4-7-3R Expressing contrast
3. g; 4. c; 5. b; 6. h; 7. d; 8. e; 9. j

4-7-4R Asking for information
3. i; 4. g; 5. f; 6. e; 7. b; 8. c; 9. h; 10. a

4-7-5R Under human control or not
3. が; 4. が; 5. を; 6. が; 7. が; 8. が; 9. を; 10. が

4-7-6R Preferred word order

3. C-A-B; 4. B-A-C; 5. A-C-B; 6. B-A-C; 7. A-C-B

4-7-7W Fill-in-the-blank

3. X; 4. を; 5. が; 6. が; 7. が; 8. が; 9. が; 10. に; 11. も; も; 12. から; まで

4-7-8W Sentence completion

3. おいしくありません; 4. おいしくありませんでした; 5. よくないです; 6. よくなかっ
たです; 7. きれいじゃありません; 8. きれいじゃありませんでした; 9. ないです;
10. なかったです

聞いてみよう *Kiite miyoo* Listening comprehension

1. a. that it's old; b. it was beautiful; 2. a. Hawaii; b. it was very beautiful; c. he brought her back some macadamia nuts from Hawaii; 3. a. what they should eat; b. cheesecake; c. to order two cheesecakes; 4. a. Yamada-san; b. five days; c. that Sato-san is coming today; 5. a. when he made the design; b. the day before yesterday; c. that it was hard to make; 6. a. when is the event next week?; b. on Wednesday, the 8th, at 7:30 p.m.; d. that it's at the Marriott Hotel; 7. a. sociology; b. math, physics, and engineering; 8. a. last Saturday; b. Giovanni, new, Italian, a bit expensive.

読んでみよう *Yonde miyoo* Contextualized reading

(1) a. for leaving early today; b. will arrive around 7:30 tomorrow
(2) a. tomorrow's meeting; b. which room to use and whether it is the usual room (#201); c. the Nihon Hotel was used for last month's meeting; d. it was a little expensive, but it was rather good.
(3) a. it is from 1:30 (not 1:00); b. from page 23 to 27 in the book
(4) a. Kyoto; b. tomorrow from 9:00 a.m.; c. Watanabe and Tanaka from Watanabe's company and Haruno and Watanuki from ZONI; d. because he was raised outside of Japan
(5) a. next semester's schedule and the location for Korean class

書き取り Dictation

1. どれがいいですか。
2. どこがおいしいですか。
3. どれができますか。

4. どれをしますか。
5. これはいくらですか。
6. あちらはどなたですか。
7. ここにはありますが、あそこにはありません。
8. ここからあそこまで、どのぐらいかかりますか。

書いてみよう Contextualized writing

1. このコピーはどこにありますか。
2. これをp．３９までコピーしました。どうぞ。
3. これはだれがコピーしましたか。いつ（コピー）しましたか。

知ってる? *Shitte'ru?* What do you know?

1	A	11	C	21	A
2	B	12	B	22	B
3	B	13	A	23	C
4	A	14	A	24	C
5	B	15	C	25	B
6	A	16	B	26	B
7	C	17	A	27	C
8	C	18	B	28	A
9	A	19	B	29	B
10	B	20	C	30	C

Act 5

5-1-1C Identifying 〜て forms
3. i; 4. g; 5. e; 6. k; 7. c; 8. a; 9. b; 10. m

5-2-1C What does Sakamoto-san want to do?
3. g; 4. a; 5. e; 6. f; 7. b; 8. d

5-3-1C How many are there?
3. six; 4. four; 5. one; 6. eight; 7. six

5-3-2C How polite is it?
Most polite: 3; Next most polite: 1; Third most polite: 4; Least polite: 2

5-4-1C What's going on?

3. b; 4. a; 5. a; 6. b; 7. b; 8. a; 9. b; 10. a

5-4-2C What's the location?

3. c; 4. h; 5. g; 6. d; 7. f; 8. e; 9. i; 10. a

5-5-1C What's going on?

3. a; 4. a; 5. b; 6. a; 7. b; 8. b; 9. b; 10. a

5-5-2CP What would you say?

3. b; 4. a; 5. c; 6. c

5-5-3CP Inviting Sakamoto-sensei to events

3. ◯; 4. ◯; 5. ✘; 6. ◯

5-6-1C What are the appointment details?

3. Professor Shirai; tomorrow after the first hour; 4. Kawamura-san, a senior student; Wednesday next week before the second hour; 5. fifteen minutes before the meeting; meeting room; 6. now; first floor lounge

5-7-1R Introducing oneself

3. Kia; 4. Keith Oscar; 5. Kirk Arthur

5-7-2R Seeking information about things and events

3. e; 4. a; 5. g; 6. b; 7. f

5-7-3R Correcting information

3. b; 4. c; 5. d

5-7-4R Asking for permission

3. b; 4. c; 5. d

5-7-5R Thank-you memos

3. e; 4. a; 5. b; 6. c

5-7-6R Identifying an odd item

3. タクシー; 4. シカゴ; 5. チケット; 6. デイジー

5-7-7W Making a shopping list

チーズケーキ、ステーキソース

5-7-8W Writing down names

3. ケニー・クック; 4. コートニー・ゲイツ; 5. デニス・ウエスト

聞いてみよう Listening comprehension

1. a. if it's OK to bring them tomorrow; b. it's fine; c. that he brings them tomorrow at the latest; 2. a. whether he can play it or not; b. that he can, with just some practice; c. yes; 3. a. now; b. by the afternoon; c. all of it; d. he says to rely on him to get it done; 4. a. for relying on him to do the job; b. take a look at it; c. it's beautiful; 5. a. to the bookstore on the eighth floor; b. it starts at 11:00; c. whether he'll return in time for the meeting; d. he'll hurry to the bookstore and return before the meeting starts; 6. a. that he'll come to it; b. next week; c. if it's OK if he doesn't come; d. she asks if he has something else to do; 7. a. reading and writing, it has gotten difficult; b. they review together; c. that they review together as soon as possible; d. when would be good; e. he says anytime is fine with him, that either today or tomorrow would be good; 8. a. if they have any questions; b. to turn in their homework by next Tuesday; c. they don't have to do it; d. because #8 is difficult; 9. a. she's improved; b. for playing tennis with her today; 10. a. if she can write with the pen she has; b. because it's hard to write with that pen; c. the pen she has.

読んでみよう Contextualized reading

(1) a. Texas; b. Isaac Carter; c. Kate, South Dakota
(2) a. coat; b. socks; c. V-neck

書き取り Dictation

1. だれがテニスしますか。
2. ツイッターはしません。
3. タクシーでいらっしゃいますか。
4. そのセーター、いくらですか。
5. あれ、タイガー・ウッズじゃありませんか?
6. あのかわいいスカート、いくらでしょうか。
7. そのノートはカーターさんのデスクにありました。
8. デザートはチーズケーキでもいいでしょうか。

書いてみよう Contextualized writing

1. クックさん
   このツアー、よかったらいらしてください。

2. ウエストさん
   あしたはタクシーでいらっしゃってください・いらしていただけますか。
3. カーターさん
   このノート、カーターさんのじゃありませんか。

知ってる? What do you know?

1	A	11	C	21	C
2	C	12	C	22	A
3	A	13	B	23	A
4	B	14	A	24	C
5	B	15	C	25	B
6	A	16	B	26	B
7	B	17	A	27	A
8	C	18	C	28	
9	B	19	A	29	
10	B	20	C	30	

Act 6

6-1-1C Ongoing action vs. resulting state
3. OA; 4. OA; 5. OA; 6. RS; 7. RS; 8. RS; 9. OA; 10. RS; 11. OA; 12. OA; 13. RS; 14. OA

6-1-2C What's going on?
3. a; 4. a; 5. a; 6. b; 7. a; 8. b; 9. b; 10. a

6-2-1C Where is it?
3. Uchida-san—behind; 4. post office—right; 5. park—next to; 6. hotel—in front

6-2-2C Point in time or amount of time?
3. A; 4. P; 5. A; 6. A; 7. P; 8. A; 9. A; 10. A; 11. P

6-3-1C More or already?
3. more; 4. more; 5. already; 6. more; 7. already; 8. more

6-3-2C Who is it?
3. a; 4. e; 5. h; 6. f

6-4-1C Listening for contact information

office room number: 502; office phone number: 63-5741; mobile phone number: 090-4277-6585; email address: otani.92@tokyo.edu

6-5-1C What's going on?

2-1. d; 2-2. c; 3-1. f; 3-2. e; 4-1. g; 4-2. h

6-6-1C Identifying question word + か & も

3. d; 4. a; 5. c; 6. d; 7. d; 8. a; 9. d; 10. a; 11. d; 12. b, 13. d; 14. c; 15. c; 16. a; 17. b; 18. b; 19. c; 20. b

6-7-1R Ordering food

3. meal; 4. meal and dessert; 5. drink

6-7-2R Verifying where people are from

3. Bennett; Minnesota; 4. Barney; Mississippi; 5. McIntire; Ireland; 6. Barnard; West Virginia

6-7-3R Asking for permission

3. starting (it) tomorrow; 4. not doing test tomorrow; 5. doing training for part-time workers the day after tomorrow

6-7-4R Politely indicating where people are

3. Lewis; Colorado; 4. Thomas; Seattle; 5. Scott; Los Angeles; 6. Garcia; Washington D.C.; 7. Edwards; Kentucky; 8. Thompson; Arkansas; 9. Rodriguez; Pennsylvania; 10. Gonzales; San Francisco; 11. Roosevelt; Missouri (St. Louis); 12. Anderson; Oregon (Portland)

6-7-5R Making requests

3. j; 4. a; 5. f; 6. b; 7. c; 8. k; 9. h; 10. i; 11. d

6-7-6R Stating what people are doing right now

3. Campbell-san; jogging over there; 4. Johnson-san; studying at the library; 5. Charles-san; watching news on the Internet; 6. Stewart-san; talking with Hugh-san in the lobby; 7. Nelson-san; watching a documentary on TV; 8. Richardson-san; eating lunch at the restaurant; 9. Harris-san; buying juice and chocolate; 10. White-san; backing up the data from the computer; 11. Jackson-san; doing an interview in a hotel in New York

6-7-7R Identifying an odd item

3. ミュージカル; 4. シンガポール; 5. サンフランシスコ; 6. ビバリー

6-7-8W Checking if something has been done already

3. アップしていません; 4. メールしていません; 5. カバ—していません; 6. プリントしていません; 7. チェックしていません

6-7-9W Getting to know new people

3. チャン・キム；ソウル；ウィンタースポーツ（スキー・スノボー）；4. ジョン・スミス；ニューヨーク；ミュージカル

聞いてみよう Listening comprehension

1. a. which person is Brian; b. he's not in the photo because he was the one who was taking the photo; 2. a. Brian; b. he's in the back, the third person from the left; c. that he's Japanese; d. she says he's Chinese-American; e. his aikido rank; f. he hasn't achieved first rank yet; he's pretty good at it; 3. a. that a student from the U.S. is doing a homestay at his home; b. because she already knows about the student; c. they were students at the same university but not in the same Japanese class; d. they haven't seen each other for five months, but they've been texting each other; 4. a. he's trying to reach someone who works at Yoshida Shipping; b. she met that person last week and was given their business card; c. because the phone number he has is different from the one on the business card; d. that the card he has is old and that she has the new one; 5. Sasha's report at the planning meeting this morning; b. she wanted to do a better job; c. that even the company president was listening to the report; 6. a. to leave right after the meeting this afternoon; b. because she has an appointment at the medical clinic; c. because the doctor is very busy and so it's hard to schedule an appointment; d. that she's not well; 7. a. 7:00 on Wednesday; b. the name of the restaurant; c. 'Midori' is the name of the restaurant; it's a female name as well as a color; d. right between the station and the office; 8. a. eat more; b. she's had enough; c. that she hasn't eaten one of the dishes; d. she says that she has eaten it; 9. a. consult with Sasha Morris before turning it in; b. if she's in a rush; c. she'd like to decide everything in one week's time; 10. a. if the color is okay; b. that brown would be better; c. because the top part is yellow, brown would show up more clearly; d. that it wouldn't be interesting; e. she disapproves.

読んでみよう Contextualized reading

(1) a. all classes are recommended; Would you like to exercise together? b. free (open to all) swimming, baby swimming, water aerobics; c. yoga, pilates, aerobics, hula dance, jazz dance, stretch, and machine training.
(2) a. Ocean View; b. ¥450; c. tomato, onion; d. sea food salad; e. pasta carbonara f. vegetable sandwich; g. vanilla, strawberry, chocolate

書き取り Dictation

1. レベッカ・ロバーツ/ニューメキシコ/アイスクリーム
2. ジュリア・ルーカス/メリーランド/ヨガ
3. ブリジット・ホワイト/ケンタッキー/バスケットボール
4. ジャック・ロペス/マサチューセッツ/カメラ
5. ジョン・サックス/ノースキャロライナ/アップルパイ
6. ビル・カーター/ユタ/ミュージカル

書いてみよう Contextualized writing

1. スミスさんはまだチェックしていませんけど、アルバイトのスケジュール、どうぞ。
2. このコンピュータ(ー)、もうだめですからリサイクルしてください。
3. キャサリンさん
   あのレストランのメニューです。ここのパスタはどれもすごくおいしいですよ。

知ってる? What do you know?

1	A	11	B	21	A	31	A
2	B	12	C	22	C		
3	B	13	B	23	C		
4	C	14	A	24	B		
5	A	15	B	25	B		
6	B	16	C	26	A		
7	C	17	C	27	B		
8	A	18	B	28	B		
9	C	19	B	29	C		
10	B	20	B	30	B